A Natural Year

by
GRACE FIRTH

Simon and Schuster · New York

To my mother
Veronica Kabureck Ushler

ACKNOWLEDGMENTS

I SHOULD LIKE to take this opportunity to thank friends and kin who have kindly helped me with ideas, recipes and advice. My thanks are also due to the Fairfax County, Virginia, librarians, the staff at the Library of Congress, and the Cooperative Extension Service workers, U.S. Department of Agriculture in Culpeper County, Virginia, in cooperation with Virginia Polytechnic Institute, Blacksburg, Virginia. The Home Economics Extension Service, U.S. Department of Agriculture, of Calvert County, Maryland, together with the Cooperative Extension Service, University of Maryland, College Park, Maryland, have been most helpful.

In addition I would like to express my gratitude to Ellen Anderson and Nelle Haber for their friendly and practical assistance.

Above all I am grateful to all who guided my early training and to my family who patiently try to understand my idiosyncrasies.

Contents of This Volume

7

Contents of This Volume

IV
Mountains of Herring and Hen Fruit
with Oceans of Oysters and Greens
APRIL

Moon lore of Aries. Gardening by the moon, temperatures and time. Wild potherbs: pepper-grass, pennycress, mustard. Oysters, keeping in bushel, oysters and new greens, Eskimo oysters, oyster frills, pickled oysters. Herring: deviled, stewed, marinated, pickled, in sour cream. Smoking fish, hot and cold methods. Native smoked herring. Eggs preserved in wax and salted. Eskimos and eggs. April and eggs as symbols of hope.

V
The Earth Blooms
MAY

Moon in Taurus and garden tools. Transplanting seedlings, seeding leafy "neck vegetables": chard, endive, lettuce, spinach. Plant melons, cucumbers, pole beans, limas and corn. Potatoes, carrots, beets and peanuts by the dark of Taurus. Cultivate during fourth quarter. Stagger plantings. Wild foods: strawberries, morel mushrooms, and sprouts of poke, milkweed, asparagus and bracken. Flower wines: daisy, honeysuckle, rose. Roses: in tea, preserving, pickled buds. Sachets, insect deterrents, rose jar. Bees, honey remedies, mead with blossoms and pineapple. May brings warmth.

VI
Age of Elders
JUNE

Gemini, cultivate earth and destroy weeds. The moon in Cancer, productive for planting. Pregnant moon. Fishing and turtle, fricassee and soup. Catch-cropping. Summer Christmas and bugs; ditch oil and naphthalene, tobacco, kerosene, soapy water, Bordeaux, sulphur, pyrethrum, rotenone and "baccy" juice. Household insect repellents. Garden peas for canning and drying; squash; rhubarb for soufflé, pie and wine. June berries in relish and dried. Mulberries in pie, jam and juice. Cherry conserve. Wild foods: lamb's-quarters; daylily buds; elder blooms in wine, in fritters, and as capers. The power of elders in June.

VII
Time of Berries
JULY
page 115

Weather predictions by moon phases. Cancer plantings and Leo chores: onions broken, asparagus set by, tomatoes fertilized; stagger corn and cucumbers. Eat new potatoes, squash, green beans, chard, beets, corn. Can green beans. Wild berries of the *Rubus* family: baked-appleberry, thimbleberry, dew-, black-, and blueberries in wine, cordials, jam, pies, and preserved by drying. Winter teas: sweet birch, sassafras, spicebush, elder leaves. A-frogging and trading in July.

VIII
The Beautiful World of Fruit
AUGUST
page 133

Lunar gardening. Under Leo, dry and can, pickle and brine: sauerkraut, dry corn, potted corn, hominy. Applesauce and skin wine, fried apples. Peaches brandied, candied and canned. Plums in kuchen and preserves. Wild foods: groundnuts, mayapples in jam, fox grapes in jam, pawpaw bread; and elderberries, canned, dried, fritters and wine. Milkweed pods and puffballs. Iced teas: birch, sumac, mint and nettle. Root beer. Contemplating the earth's goodness on an August afternoon.

Contents of This Volume

Contents of This Volume

mincemeat. Sagittarius heralds butchering season: slaughter, scald; carcass cleaned, cut up. Pork: dry sugar-cure method, packing, overhauling, drying bacon, sausage making, canning sausage. Lard making, crackling bread. Soap making. Variety meats: headcheese, scrapple, spicy times in November.

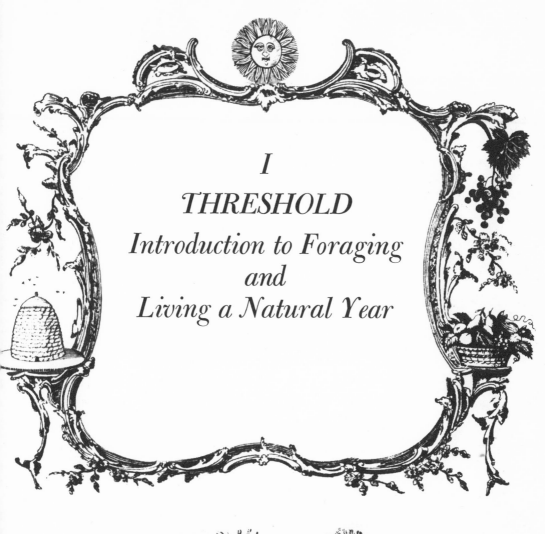

I
THRESHOLD
Introduction to Foraging
and
Living a Natural Year

MY FIRST REAL-LIFE ENCOUNTER with the charm and challenge of wild foods developed spontaneously.

Our boat sank.

The sinking was not a dramatic, tail-up, movie-type demise; rather, our overburdened, untrustworthy craft simply settled to the bottom of Mary's Cove, an isolated bite of the North Pacific east of Cain's Head, Alaska.

As our provisions and gear burped their last gasps we dove into the bubbles but succeeded in retrieving only one gun and two funny books before the chill of the May evening drove us ashore. By great good fortune and one companion's fine memory we found an abandoned cabin complete with four bunks, a pipeless stove, two tins of rusty flour and a jar of caked sourdough.

My status as cook of our now defunct bear-reconnaissance mission prompted me to add water to the encrusted yeast and to bring it with me to my bunk with a chink-hole view. I had heard of yeast plants living for years in a dormant stage and knew that if I could rejuvenate the antique sourdough, life on that remote beach would be easier.

We were thrilled the next morning to find that not only had the soggy weather passed and we were in an enchantingly pleasant bay, but best of all, my body-warmed sourdough showed signs of life. As tiny blurps of activity broke its surface my companions whooped for hotcakes. The starter had to grow before it could be used, so hotcakes were temporarily forsaken.

Instead we turned to the sea for food: mussels, crabs, rock oysters, urchins, shrimp, little fish. I had never really looked at the ocean before, really looked at the bounty of the beach. My forte had been the land. From early childhood I was my grandfather's partner on foraging trips. So while the two men

15

stalked shrimp with a shirt stretched between two poles, I cruised the bushes. Actually I hadn't left the high-water drift before I found breakfast: sorrel, goosetongue, sea-rockets and a battered bucket. With our waterproof matches I started a beach fire and soon had water boiling for greens and shrimp: our first foraged meal.

Our encounter with nature lasted eleven days: eleven adventurous days of misshapen fry bread cooked on hot rocks, seafowl eggs, clams, roots, greens and sand-shark steak. Then a Scandinavian freighter, alerted by a Coast Guard "overdue" dispatch, maneuvered into Mary's Cove, lowered a boat, and eight bearded, turtlenecked seamen rowed ashore to rescue us. My companions tried to drag me into the bushes to hide; they didn't want to be saved. We had fared well on the bounty of the northland.

Two other experiences in my carefree Alaskan days knock at the half-forgotten forager's chambers of my innermost mind. Once on an attempted takeoff from a desolate sandbar in the interior, our plane nosed over and the propeller broke. My companion and I could either have sat there and whittled a new prop or walked out. We chose to whittle, and while my friend carved I browsed the area much as I'd browse in a market. During the four days we whittled we never missed a meal. We ate blueberries by the handful, parsnip roots, willow buds and rhubarb, fern fiddles, fibers, greens—and gorgeous mushrooms. The only thing we really missed was salt. We had the opposite end of our propeller shaped to balance the broken side when Air Rescue spotted us.

The last time I lived off the land out of need was in southeastern Alaska. Stormbound at Redoubt Bay for seven days, we ate fish, fowl, fresh salad, fruit, blossoms, buds, bulbs, stems and seeds. "Everywhere is food!" my Indian friend remarked, for he also had been reared to live in harmony with the land.

My introduction to wild foods, gardening, preserving, baking and wine making, was a casual one. I lived with my grandparents in Connecticut and Missouri, and Uncle Steve, as everyone called my grandfather, could make food out of anything. I foraged, fished, hoed, baked and brewed right along with him and didn't realize that the rest of the world was not doing the same.

Marriage brought babies, bottles and diapers, but when they were behind me, I turned again to the life I remembered. It was not a "return."

Actually I live a comfortable suburban life: an old frame house, a husband with an eight-to-five job, three teen-age children who enjoy prowling for puffballs, pickling pears, camping, tramping and eating half-pound hamburgers. We five are always ready for fun. And gardening, gathering, preserving, as well as satisfying robust appetites, can be a great deal of fun.

Each scene is different; each season and year highlights a different offering: the time we caught a snapper, or vice versa; the day we scrounged blackberries and dug up a still; the evening we captured some pears and yellow jackets liberated them from us; the autumn we stewed squirrel in buckshot gravy; the winter we swapped persimmon pudding for wine sausage; the June we harvested elder blow in a bull pasture and almost ended up on the horns of a dilemma. All these are treasured family memories.

Foraging is a family hobby which may be pursued along old railroad tracks, in swamps and fields, beside streams and fence rows, on beaches and roadsides, and around abandoned farms. Foraging is an experience in which one feels the pulse of the earth.

Gardening takes a plot of land, a hoe and willing muscles. Scratching the soil, harvesting garden fruits, are peaceful pursuits. With a garden, there is hope.

Preserving and wine making require a few jars and bottles,

some surplus food, and fruit with "heat" in it. Preserving the bounty of nature is an act of faith. To save is to say that there will be a tomorrow.

Foraging, gardening, using and saving God's gifts blend with elegant simplicity into a natural year.

II
Time of Seeding and Yeast
FEBRUARY

Moon under Aquarius and Pisces. Prediction of
summer weather. Pisces seeding and planters for
cabbage, eggplant, peppers and tomatoes. A fixed
order of life. Wild foods: Jerusalem artichokes and
slippery elm. Yeasts: potato and sourdough starters.
Bread baking. Sourdough hot cakes and fry bread.
Dark breads: bean and acorn. Home-brew beer.
Root wines: potato, beet, carrot, "mulligan stew."
Vinegar. February, the time to awaken.

Iᴛ ᴀʟʟ sᴛᴀʀᴛs in February.

Primitive peoples, who held a real interest in the natural cycle of food-getting, looked on February as the beginning. Such native names as "Seeds Swell," "First Things Are Born," "River Mothers Grow Big" indicate this.

My grandfather set store by Indian legends and signs. He believed that the position of the moon during the first two weeks of February indicated whether the growing season would be wet or dry. If the horns pointed down at that time, my grandfather said it meant that "the moon was emptying its water," and that the following spring and summer would be wet. The type of seed he selected and the location of the crops in his garden were determined by the early February moon's wet or dry prediction. A dry February moon—one with the horns pointing up—influenced him to plant his garden as early as possible and to use drought-resistant seeds.

Grandaddy prepared the seeding-frame soil early in February under the zodiac sign of Aquarius because he said dry or barren signs were best for turning sod. He also said that the last quarter of the moon was best for preparing the soil for cultivation. So when the February moon under Aquarius "looked like a dog tooth" he spaded his seeding frames in preparation for tomato, cabbage and other seeds.

If the new moon rode in under Aquarius' February days, it was predicted that crops would be poor because of blight or insects. Conversely, if the full moon occurred during February 1 to February 19, it was believed that the following summer's gardens would thrive.

Astrologers teach that the twelve signs of the zodiac are dominated by specific tendencies and characteristics which influence all growing things. Aquarius (January 20 to February 19) is believed to be dominated by airy and dry tendencies and barren and masculine characteristics. Therefore planting under Aquarius is not generally recommended.

Pisces (February 19 to March 21) is considered a highly fruitful zodiac sign. Under Pisces the moon emerges above the plane of the earth's orbit and is "good for planting," my grandfather said. Pisces holds watery, feminine and productive characteristics, and astrologers aver that it is the best sign under which to make seeding-frame plantings.

I must admit that I feel stirrings with the first warmth of spring. I don't know whether it is the moon or the seed catalogs that stirs my sap and inspires me to start sawing milk cartons in half for windowsill seeding.

There are many ideas for seeding frames, but I use milk cartons cut the long way with holes poked in the bottom of one of the halves. The planter half with the holes is placed inside the other half, which catches the drip. The planter part is filled with one handful of compost plus two of sand. Seedlings, like children, need lots of nutrients and sand makes root pruning simpler. Although I start planning my garden early in February, I do not plant seeds in windowsill boxes until the latter part of the month.

Most seedlings should be ready to plant permanently in approximately ten weeks, so if you follow the moon-sign lore, start your indoor seedlings under the sign of Pisces.

Traditionally, cabbage seeds are started indoors first and last. A mild-flavored, early variety for slaw and kraut should be seeded about the last week of February, moon willing. Later, a winter variety is planted for "keeping" cabbage.

Eggplant and peppers grow slowly and are set out later in the season, so they should be seeded after cabbage. Eggplants are remunerative for the effort involved, and sweet peppers are always a surprise—suddenly lush peppers seem to pop into focus. They both grow readily in windowsill boxes and produce late in the garden season when appetites for regular garden fare seem to pale.

Brussels sprouts and broccoli are vigorous seedlings although I have not had much B & B happiness because either the drought, heat, cool weather, dampness, disease or wild life gets them.

For the fun of it, I've tried starting beans, squash and corn indoors, but, though they grow like crazy, they become leggy and are nearly impossible to transplant.

Tomato-seed plantings should be staggered in order to insure fruit all summer. I like to plant about four varieties of tomatoes: early, main crop, a low-acid yellow variety, and one late bearer for canning. Direct seeding into the soil is recommended by some gardeners but I always lose the seedlings in the weeds. One year I dutifully cut down all my plants and left fine straight rows of baby ragweed. Tomato seedlings and windowsills go together. It's psychologically satisfying to see tomatoes grow. Some people even wait until the fruit is set on their early seedlings before they transplant them into the garden. My grandfather waited until the ladybugs arrived before setting out tomatoes. He said ladybugs were a tomato's best friend.

Starting vegetables indoors from seed may seem to be an unthrifty use of time, but the emotional advantages outweigh the practical aspects of purchasing commercial plants. For one thing, the cycle is complete: a family chooses seed, sows, transplants, cultivates, harvests and preserves. Living seedlings on a sunny windowsill keep a family in touch with nature. The waiting and watching may be likened to a gestation period: a time of preparation. The garden plot should be plowed, tested, fertilized and cultivated during this period. A fixed order of life emerges.

Although there are not many wild foods to harvest in February, there is the Jerusalem artichoke (*Helianthus tuberosus*). Midday, when the ground is thawed, dig where you have noted old artichoke canes; the tuber parts to be eaten grow two to four inches below the surface and are scattered within a foot radius of the cane. The sunflower *Helianthus* plant, which is six to ten feet tall, should be identified in late September or in October when it blooms. Jerusalem artichokes are American natives and bear rough, toothed leaves, which grow opposite each other at the base of the plant, but bear alternate leaves higher up on their hairy stems. A trio of yellow daisy flowers two to three inches in diameter sprouts near the upper leaves.

I have seen Jerusalem artichokes growing in moist soil along roadsides throughout the northeastern and north central states. Many suburban stream banks are cluttered with the leggy plants.

When you have identified Jerusalem artichokes, it is best to mark the spot in the fall. Then, just before spring, follow the old canes into the earth. *Helianthus tuberosus* are best after they have been frosted and they do not keep more than two or three weeks after they have been dug. The tubers are "like pigeon eggs," an old cookbook states. Some pigeon! The roots I've gathered are numerous under each plant and often run two inches in circumference and four inches long. Digging does not seem to harm the plant. In fact, the four tubers I planted amid my husband's strawberries have multiplied in spite of our digging until now he can't find the strawberries.

French cooks wash and peel Jerusalem artichokes, cube them, and simmer them gently in butter for ten minutes, or until almost done. They season with pepper and salt, cover them with a thin cream sauce made with a roux of two tablespoons of butter, one tablespoon of flour, one cup of milk and one cup of cream, a sprig of thyme, a little grated nutmeg, pepper and salt. The artichokes are cooked as slowly as possible in the cream sauce and served in a deep dish.

We like Jerusalem artichokes simply blanched in boiling water for three minutes, peeled, then boiled until soft, drained and served with butter, salt and pepper.

Artichokes do not crisp well when fried, but they cook

quickly in a skillet of ham drippings or butter, and disappear at the table just as fast.

I put them in Chinese food at the last moment in place of water chestnuts, and they are crunchy with a nutty flavor. I have also used them in bread dressing heated briefly under an already cooked breast of turkey. Cooked for only five or ten minutes, the artichokes retain their natural crisp sweetness. When used in regular turkey stuffing, however, they disintegrate and can't be found. Also, their taste becomes stronger when they have been cooked for a longer period of time and overrides other flavors.

A purée of Jerusalem artichokes may be made by simmering them briefly in water and rubbing them through a sieve. The purée may be used in soufflés, in casseroles with bread crumbs and cheese, or blended with mashed potatoes. Some gourmets prefer them glazed and baked like candied sweet potatoes.

A salad of Jerusalem artichokes may be made like potato salad, or the raw artichokes may be diced and tossed in a green salad. Raw, they have a placid root taste that is sometimes described as "wild." Their flavor is quite different from other food flavors and should not be compared to familiar foods.

For that matter, there are few wild foods that taste like store-bought foods. It is an error to embrace foraging with the attitude of comparison. Each food is individual. Wild foods have their own flavors, feel and fragrance. Just as new friends must be met and savored with respect, new foods must be treated as individuals. To try to force wild-food flavors into familiar taste categories is a mistake. Jerusalem artichokes are different and should be tasted on their own merit.

There has been some literature on the Jerusalem artichoke as a food for diabetics because of its low calorie content and its sugar-conversion qualities, but the U.S. Department of Agriculture warns that little is presently known about the diet value of this root.

As a vegetable, sunroot, as the Indians called the Jerusalem artichoke, has challenged cooks since Pilgrim times. Artichokes awaken new appetites, it is true, but to me one of the pleasures of this plant comes from scratching Mother Earth early each spring in search of her first fruits.

Years ago, loggers were busy during February, and my grandfather and I used to invade recently logged-out woodlots in search of the slippery elm (*Ulmus fulva*). The name for this tree, common to fertile soils of northern United States and parts of Canada, comes from the slippery inner bark, the part that may be eaten. Inner bark of other elms may be eaten, but *Fulva* is less tough and bitter. The slippery, a medium-sized elm, is identified by its rough, hairy twigs and fuzzy buds. The hairy stems are the key to slippery elm.

Although the slippery bark may be taken any time, my grandfather looked for the large branches left behind by the loggers. He cut the coarsely textured bark with his pocket-knife and it curled back to expose the slippery part. Layers of the inner bark peeled easily, and we carried the gooey stuff home, cut it into six-by-four-inch strips and laid it on paper in the attic. When dried, the hardened bark was ground in our large fly-wheel grinder, which was powered by my long arm. Then we'd all have tea. Grandma made my elm tea with milk and a bit of sugar.

I have heard that dried slippery elm can be ground into flour and used in baking or boiled into a pudding, but I do not remember eating it that way.

The literature notes that slippery elm was an early-day scurvy preventative when chewed in times of emergency. As I remember, the taste was bland and milky and the feel was decidedly slippery, but it made a warming tea to drink with popcorn on winter evenings.

What dark, dank day is not lightened by the smell of fresh-baked bread? What heart is not warmed by mellow wine?

The one-celled fungus, yeast, is another plant that is especially appreciated during the gray days of February.

There are good yeasts and bad yeasts.

Bad yeasts sour both bread and wine.

Good yeasts ferment dough and juice, and their enzymes change some of the sugars to carbon dioxide and alcohol. They also give the flour gluten an elastic texture.

Both dry yeast, which is dormant yeast plants mixed with corn meal, and compressed yeast, the yeast mass ready-mixed with starch and moisture, may be purchased in modern grocery stores. However, years ago yeasts were home grown.

Home-grown yeasts for baking fit into two categories: yeast grown with water and potatoes, called liquid yeast starter, and yeast grown in water and flour, called sourdough. Both starters utilize old yeast plants called ferments (obtained by buying commercial yeast), and they are kept growing by adding potato or flour mixtures as a yeast food substance.

Liquid yeast starter for baking may be made initially by peeling, cubing and boiling three potatoes in one-and-one-half cups of water. Cool and mash the potatoes in the water in which they were cooked. Add four tablespoons of sugar, one-and-one-half tablespoons of salt, and enough lukewarm water (82° F.) to make three-and-one-quarter cups of mushy liquid. A package of dry yeast dissolved in a cup of water is added, and the whole thing must stand in a warm place overnight.

The liquid yeast starter will silently froth and rave and make your kitchen smell like a brewery. But that can lead to interesting personality studies: I had one neighbor who entered the front door of our home and sniffed straight through each room to the kitchen where she lifted pot lids until she spotted my starter working. Another one fidgeted on the edge of her chair taking in great draughts of air and looking at me suspiciously. My Avon lady bounces in periodically "just to smell."

One cup of this liquid yeast starter is saved each time and used instead of commercial yeast to activate the potato glop the night before the next baking. Liquid yeast starter will maintain itself for a week or ten days if it is stored in a clean, loosely covered jar in a cool place. Liquid yeast starters may be used with the straight dough method of making light bread or with the sponge method.

For the straight dough method, use the three-and-one-quarter cups of liquid yeast that are left after a cup of starter has been saved, and add three tablespoons fat and five tablespoons sugar, and set this over a pan of hot water for about a half hour or until lukewarm. Add one teaspoon of salt and about ten to twelve cups of flour. The exact quantity of flour required differs according to the kind of flour and to the consistency of the liquid yeast starter. When the flour and liquid are thoroughly mixed and no longer stick to the sides of the bowl, knead by hand on a floured board. My grandmother insisted that bread should be kneaded twenty minutes by the clock.

After kneading, grease the dough and put it into a bowl to rise. The temperature should be kept at about 80° F. When the dough doubles in bulk it should be punched down for about a minute, then returned to the bowl to rise again. Two risings give bread an even texture. (If the holes in baked bread are too small, it is a sign of insufficient rising; if they are too big, it is a sign of badly kneaded dough or too much heat when rising.)

When the dough has doubled in bulk the second time, it should be divided, rounded into loaf shapes, greased, and put into greased pans for the last rising. After the loaves reach proper size, slip them into a preheated hot oven (425°–450° F.) and bake twenty to thirty minutes for a crusty one-pound loaf. For a quick tan, brush loaves with a little milk and sugar. Loaves will shrink from the sides of the pan when done.

If you wish to use the sponge method of baking light bread, activate the potato-yeast starter in the morning and that evening pour off one cup to save in a lightly covered jar. Mix half of the flour needed for a batch of bread (maybe five cups) into the remaining three-and-one-quarter cups of liquid yeast starter, cover and leave overnight in a draft-free area, 65°–75° F., to form a light sponge. In the morning it will look like the surface of the moon. The sponge should then be stirred well and salt, sugar, shortening and the rest of the flour added to make a dough. I use the same amounts and ingredients for both the straight-dough method and the sponge method of baking bread. Both doughs are mixed and handled in the same manner, and I cannot tell the difference in the product.

Two cautions I might add: remember the rising-in-the-pans step. I omitted this when telling a young lady about the wonders of bread making and she had to scrape her loaves off the roof of her oven. Also, remember to save a cup of starter for the next making before adding flour to form the sponge. I did not have my starter once, and the next morning I decided to save a cup of the sponge instead. The bread made from that latter-day odoriferous yeast was off-color and sour.

True sourdough has a wholesome acid taste. Sourdough starters were traditionally used by the *promyshlenniki*, or free-lance Russian explorers. Early Alaskans were called "Sourdoughs" because they carried a bit of this simple leavening with them in their travels.

More recent sourdough starters are made by soaking one-half package of dry yeast in one-half cup of warm water. When dissolved, mix thoroughly with an additional cup of warm water, one teaspoon of sugar and two-thirds cup flour. Keep in a warm place, and after the sourdough starter works well, stir down, sprinkle with flour and store in a cool place for two to three weeks or until ready to use. Mix a little flour and warm water into this soupy-paste yeast the night before you wish to make hotcakes and stow it behind the stove for warmth. It will work actively and become evil-smelling.

The first thing the following morning, add about a cup of the sourdough to a bowl containing warm water, a little sugar and oil and salt. Scatter flour over this slush and whip it with a fork to make a batter. Let it work in a warm place while the coffee is heating, then fry into puffy pancakes. Sourdough hotcakes made the old way are like ripe eggs—they make the fresh products seem pale by comparison.

Fry bread was originally made by simply using the sourdough starter, water, salt, grease and sugar (if available), and flour. Of course, part of the starter was set aside after it had been activated and the amount of fry bread "baked" was determined by the amount of water and flour used. Sourdough fry bread was kneaded, allowed to rise, shaped into buns and "baked." Historically, Alaskans did not bake their bread in ovens but rather cooked it in small cakes on griddles, stove tops or flat rocks near a fire. That can be pretty gritty. Gripping, too. I have heard of old-timers who used sourdough to seal lids on their stills, and of others who have patched stovepipes and rubber boots with it. In my opinion, sourdough is overrated as food.

The brownish breads that used to be made in the country were kept fresh a long time by the use of moisture-retaining and coarsely ground barley, rye or potato flour with wheat. These breads were often coarse because it was difficult to hull grains. The usual proportions were one part rye or other flour to three or four parts wheat.

Bean flours may be made by grinding dry beans either whole or with the seed coat removed. Flavorful bean breads are made by combining one part bean flour to four or five parts wheat flour.

My grandmother had an interesting brownish bean bread that was stout but pleasant. She dissolved one package of yeast in a cup of warm water, added two cups of warm milk, two tablespoons of sugar, two tablespoons of fat, four teaspoons of salt and about two cups of lima-bean flour. About eight cups of white flour tightened the dough, and it was kneaded and handled like light bread dough.

Serve lima-bean bread warm with clear ham-bone soup made by boiling one ham bone and a handful each of dried prunes, apricots, peaches, and/or apples. Drizzle a fistful of noodles into the broth about ten minutes before supper and salt-pepper to taste. The sweet-salt soup and hearty bean bread make a meal which is tasty and not difficult to prepare.

Acorn bread is traditional to pioneer America but I've never been able to try it. One year my acorns got weavils and crawled away. The following year I picked up a bushel of acorns and brought them home only to have suburban squirrels steal them from the back porch before I had my eyes open the next morning. The third year I went after acorns determined to guard them with my life and talents. But my favorite tree was gone. Some noble woodsman had seen $75 or $80 in that massive chestnut oak and had cut it down. Smashed young trees one hundred feet from its stump attested to its size and agony. I have lamented many times that I did not plant some of the thumbnail-sized seeds of that tremendous tree.

Had I been able to save proper acorns, chestnut oak acorns, *Quercus prinus*, I would have blanched the thoroughly dried kernels in several boiling-water baths until their astringent taste had gone, then dried them in a slow oven and ground them in a coarse flour. Acorn flour may be used like cornmeal in muffins or soda-baking powder breads.

Acorn light bread is made as follows: Dissolve one package of dry yeast in one cup warm water with one teaspoon sugar. Add two cups warm milk, four tablespoons of sugar, three tablespoons of shortening and four teaspoons of salt. Mix well and add four cups of acorn flour with about seven or eight cups of white flour to make a dough. Proceed as for white bread: knead, let rise, punch down, let rise, put in pans, and let rise again. Bake in pound loaves for thirty to forty minutes in a hot oven, 400° F. A pan of hot water should be placed in the oven during baking.

This recipe was given to me by an old woman whose

cheeks resembled topaz chamois and whose eyes never wavered when she told me of men—black, red and white—who, fifty years before, had fought for her favor. Sometime later, when I heard that the old woman had died, I asked a neighbor, "Was she white?" And he answered, "Round here she warn't."

During the prohibition era, home-brew beer was called "hops tea" by many suds fanciers, and my grandfather stayed with this misnomer even after 3.2 became legal. He always dedicated part of February to making "tea" in order to get ready for the hot weather. Actually home-brew beer takes only about six weeks to mature but I think he wanted to free his large crocks for the first blooms and berries of spring. I believe his heart was more with wine making than with beer.

According to my grandfather, there were two main types of malt: light and dark. Malt is barley that has sprouted and been dried and ground; germination changes the grain so that it dissolves easily. The length of time malt has been dried or roasted determines the type of malt. Light malts are used in their natural state or have been dried with a lesser degree of heat than dark malts. Light malts are used in making light, ale-type beers, and dark malt brews into stout or heavier tasting beer.

Yeast also affects the taste of beer. Uncle Steve said baker's yeast gives the flavor and head of rapid-fermenting, ale-type beers, while other strains of yeast have been cultured by brewers for different beers. I know my grandfather was covetous of his yeasts and kept his brewer's culture going by saving a little (like saving sourdough) with which to start the next batch.

Two other ingredients affect the taste of beer in addition to the actual recipe and processing: they are hops and water. My grandfather thought city water "tasted" his beer, although I have heard others claim that chlorine and other additives have no effect. Uncle Steve used well water which he drew with a hand pump in the basement. Many an hour I spent on the business end of that pump handle, and if I tarried too long between downs and ups I'd lose my prime, and it took thirteen dry pumps to get water flowing again.

"Don't lose your prime!" I would hear my grandfather calling from across the cellar when I paused to daydream a bit. And that's what I tell my young ones when they want to stop homework to watch "just one" television show.

Hops is a vine that produces a leafy conelike flower. Unfertilized cones are used in beer making to give flavor, fragrance and tannin. They also provide some yeast food and thus aid fermentation. Most of the time a handful of hops was merely tossed into the brew, but sometimes my grandfather infused hops tied in a cloth in boiling water and added it to the beer crock. Sometimes he made beer without adding hops.

As I remember his basic recipe, one cup of yeast ferment was activated with sugar and set aside (one package of yeast and one teaspoon sugar dissolved in a cup of warm water) while a three-pound can of malt extract was mixed with a bucket of warm water in a ten-gallon crock. Five pounds of sugar was stirred into the mixture and the crock was filled to within four inches of the top with tepid water. The yeast and a handful of hops were thrown in, the crock covered, and the pungent brown liquid was allowed to brew or ferment.

First it boiled up and was topped with a creamy scum. Later the brew settled and my grandfather watched it like a hungry cat watches fledglings. He used the eyeball method. Face tense and not breathing, he would stare at the surface tension of the crock a full minute. Then he'd stick his head down and listen. When the pin-drop plops were silenced and the top of the crock showed little activity, he'd sterilize bottles, get out the bottle capper and siphon his home-brew beer into bottles for sealing.

Grandaddy used to let his bottled home brew "set" for a couple of months, but in Seward, Alaska, I heard tales of drinking "quite a hole in the batch" when word got out that someone was bottling in Bootleg Alley. Six weeks seems to be considered adequate aging by those who know about such things.

A vital February chore on my grandfather's calendar was "putting down roots." Translated, that meant culling vegetables from the root racks in the cellar and making wine from any parsnips, potatoes, beets, carrots, or turnips which he considered surplus.

With my small garden and eager eaters I never have surplus, but I have experimented with marked-down potatoes and other slightly shopworn produce. I substituted one package of yeast dissolved in one cup of water for a cup of Uncle Steve's yeast ferment.

Potato wine was my grandmother's favorite, and she kept a cruet of it on the table for her evening toddy. It is reminiscent of a musty Rhine wine, somewhat dry, dulcet, and equally excellent for cooking or nipping. It possesses neither dramatic color nor fragrance but it is the workhorse of root wines, just as grape is the backbone of fruit wines.

Wash and chop about one gallon of old potatoes (skins included), add one package of raisins and four thinly sliced lemons. Toss them all into a five-gallon crock or plastic wastebasket. Boil two gallons of water in which five pounds of sugar have been dissolved and pour over the potato mixture. Stir well and when lukewarm mix in one package of dry yeast which has been softened in a cup of warm water. Cover and set in a warm place for two weeks. Strain through several cloths, allow it to settle, then siphon into sterilized bottles. Cork lightly, pushing down the corks every day or so. When the corks stay down, ram them home to seal. Place bottles on their sides in a darkened area and try not to use this wine until the following spring because potato wine improves with age.

In flavor and appearance, beet wine is the opposite of that made with potatoes. Exquisitely beautiful, winsome yet voluptuous, it graces a dinner table with its crystal-clear fuchsia, but to my taste beet wine is rather insipid. Its redeeming factors are its looks and alcoholic content. I've known people like that—not much depth, but long on looks, and heady.

Boil about one-half peck of washed but unpeeled beets in two or three gallons of water. When soft, cool to lukewarm, chop the beets and dump them and their bloody water into a large crock. Stir in five pounds of sugar and one package of yeast that has been dissolved in one cup of warm water. Cover the crock and keep it at 55° to 65° F. but squeeze the beets with your hands every day or so for two weeks. Strain through a jelly bag, let settle for a few hours and siphon into sterilized bottles. Cork lightly, regularly pushing down the corks until fermentation stops. When corks stay down, decant carefully into fresh sterile bottles, leaving the sediment in the bottom of the old bottles. Cork and seal by dripping paraffin over each cork.

I have heard of people adding crushed ginger root, stick cinnamon, cloves or peppercorns to beet wine to give it zip, but I have not tried it.

Carrot wine is surprising. It has a richness and color you wouldn't believe—golden as a summer sunset and full-bodied as bouillon made with two hens. I used to visualize nutrients soaring through my veins after a sip or two.

Chop and boil about five pounds of old carrots (all green removed) in two-and-one-half gallons of water until soft. Squeeze through a cloth and add five pounds of sugar, one-half dozen cut-up unpeeled oranges, a pound of muscat raisins and a few pieces of bruised ginger root or stem to the pulpy liquid. Set aside until lukewarm; then add one package of dry yeast which has been dissolved in one cup of warm water. Cover the crock and let it work in a warm place for two weeks, stirring frequently, strain and finally siphon into sterilized bottles and cork lightly. Lift, then push down the corks every day and, when fermentation has stopped, seal tightly with a hard thrust of the cork. This wine will change from brick to amber while retaining the bloom of muscat and the glow of orange, with overtones of ginger. Beautiful beverage!

I have made this with four pounds of brown sugar instead of five pounds of white, forgotten it, then served it after black-eyed peas and hog jowl, a provocative toast to New Year's promises.

With all the leftover roots Uncle Steve made "mulligan stew" a lively, flavorful, soft-as-velvet drink in which his friends insisted, "Steve had put his soul."

One gallon total of chopped parsnips, carrots, turnips and whole beets are washed and boiled in two-and-one-half gallons of water until soft. When lukewarm, the vegetables are squeezed and discarded and one cake of yeast which has been dissolved in one cup of warm water is added. Five pounds of sugar, six raw apples, three potatoes, two oranges, all unpeeled, all chopped, are dropped into the elixir of vegetables and yeast. A piece of ginger root is beaten with a wooden mallet and popped into the stew along with any old raisins, figs or prunes you might have on hand.

The mulligan is covered and periodically stirred and pressed with a wooden paddle for two weeks. It is then strained and the fruits are thrown away. The liquid is allowed to settle for a day and the clear juice is siphoned off and bottled. Each container is corked lightly after a small piece of ginger is added, and when fermentation has stopped and the corks stay down, it is sealed. It is best to wait until after the spring holy days to sample with a friend.

My grandfather did not use kegs for root wines because he did not consider beverages made from a substance other than grapes as being wine. Also, as he rarely made more than two or three gallons of each root wine, bottles were more appropriate. I have halved most of his recipes and I get three or four quarts of each kind. I use plastic buckets for wine making; they are light and easy to handle. I don't know what my grandfather would have said about plastic, because he felt crocks "breathed." I use plastic bags held tight by string and elastic bands as crock and bucket covers. I wash and sterilize all containers with boiling water. However, some people recommend the use of sodium metabisulphite (four grains to a gallon of water) as a rinse that kills "bad" yeasts. I have not had unfriendly yeasts—some fine vinegars, it's true, but these were a result of my own foolishness. Cleanliness and a watchful eye are prerequisites to dependable wine.

I have allowed wine to sour into vinegar through neglect. One year we produced twelve quarts of robust blackberry vinegar. Because vinegar bacteria can contaminate good wine, I removed the neat-looking case to the garage and someone, thinking it was wine, filched it. What a blow for honesty!

In wine making, fermentation by means of natural or commercial yeasts changes fruit sugars into alcohol and carbonic acid. When wine is sealed, the fermentation process is stopped. If air comes in contact with the wine alcohol, vinegar bacteria and wild yeasts will change it into acetic acid and vinegar is born.

Vinegar manufacturers encourage *Mycoderma aceti*, or vinegar yeasts, to grow, but home brewers frown on them. My grandfather would permit no strange yeasts in his cellar. He did contend, however, that all yeasts attain more vigor under the watery and fruitful signs of the zodiac. He said that February under Pisces was a time when yeasts and seeds beg to be allowed to grow. Roots stir in the knocking wind beckoning the earth to awaken, he said, and all life yearns for the returning sun.

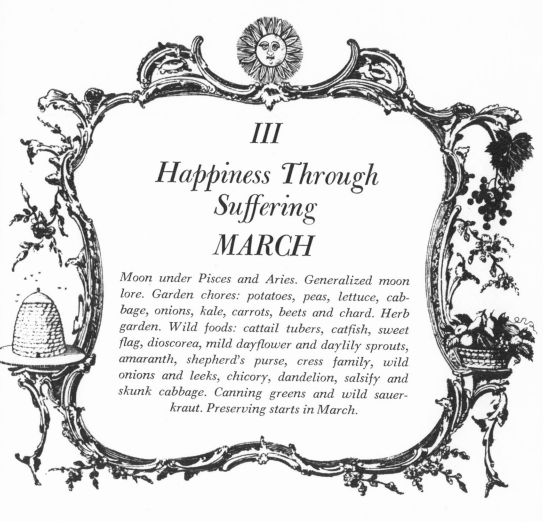

III
Happiness Through Suffering
MARCH

Moon under Pisces and Aries. Generalized moon lore. Garden chores: potatoes, peas, lettuce, cabbage, onions, kale, carrots, beets and chard. Herb garden. Wild foods: cattail tubers, catfish, sweet flag, dioscorea, mild dayflower and daylily sprouts, amaranth, shepherd's purse, cress family, wild onions and leeks, chicory, dandelion, salsify and skunk cabbage. Canning greens and wild sauerkraut. Preserving starts in March.

GARDEN CHORES for March are numerous and unpleasant, but, as Dostoevsky pointed out, happiness is earned through suffering, so I brace myself each year with thoughts of the good things to come and turn to my cold, wet labors.

Pisces, with its watery, fruitful, strong-rooted tendencies, extends from February 19 to March 21, when Aries, with its fiery, dry, windy and barren characteristics, takes control until April 20. Never plant anything in the barren sign of Aries, my grandfather advised. Plants "shoot to head" if seeded after March 21.

In addition to considering the twelve signs of the zodiac, many gardeners watch the four phases, or quarters, of the moon. The first and second quarters of the moon are increasing phases, that is, the moon is growing in size, and plants that produce their yield above ground are planted during these phases. The third quarter is a decreasing phase, sometimes called the "dark" of the moon, and crops that produce their yield underground are planted during this period. The fourth quarter is said to be best for pulling weeds, cultivating and turning sod.

Those who plant by the moon never plant on Sunday because this day is ruled by the sun and is considered to be dry and barren. My grandfather never planted on the first day of the new moon, or on days the moon changed quarters.

As an adjunct to the zodiac sign and the moon's phase considerations, the true believer in agricultural astrology also heeds the daily position of the moon. Every two or three days, the moon's place is ruled by a different zodiac sign. For example, April 8 is within the period ruled by Aries (March 21 to April 20). Aries is considered to be fiery, dry and barren.

But the sign that rules the moon's place on April 8 may be Libra, which is said to be moist, airy and fruitful. Thus the barren period sign of Aries may be weakened or overruled by the moon's daily place sign. Many almanacs carry a column called "Moon's Place," which notes the specific zodiac sign influencing each day of the month.

Potatoes are the first vegetables we sow each spring in our kitchen garden, and the day we select for planting is invariably raw and windy. Traditionally we wait until the dark of the moon following St. Patrick's Day. This year we studied the March moon signs in the almanac for guidance. The waning moon after March 17 occurred during the zodiac sign of Aries. "Dry and barren," not a good sign for planting. Nevertheless, we cut and dropped forty pounds of seed potatoes, eye up, into the ground.

We hardly made our seed. Although we grew healthy plants, samplings showed that we would barely dig as many potatoes as we had put in. Very disheartening. So disheartening, in fact, that Lewis, my husband, plowed under the whole patch, and if we don't have underground foragers this winter, our garden will be filled with potato sports next year. A sport—that's a volunteer which may or may not breed true. Plowed-under sports are the worst kind—they sprout everywhere.

If my grandfather had been here he would have waited to plant potatoes until the dark moon of Taurus (April 20 to May 21), for Taurus, like Pisces, is considered to be a moist and productive sign.

Along with potatoes, my March garden usually consists of early peas for the rabbits, lettuce sown broadcast to fool some of the birds, a few cabbage plants to satisfy the early butterflies, kale and spinach to take care of any lusting for greens, onion sets for green-onion eaters, and first plantings of carrots, beets and Swiss chard sown with radishes among them to show where the rows are located. If I feel in a gambling mood, I pop in some summer squash and snap beans.

MARCH

If late Virginia frosts outwit me, I am not proud—I return to seed again. I used to plant turnips; love those greens! But Lewis informed me that I had a choice: it was either him or them. A toss-up, I told him, but then I couldn't imagine a turnip, any turnip, greens and all, keeping my feet warm at night, so we don't plant turnips.

As a rule of thumb, most seeds should be covered to a depth of four times their longest dimension. Seeds may be planted deeper in sandy soils and also when sown later in the season. Clay soils require a shallower seeding. Soil above most seeds should be firmed for rapid germination. Walking on newly seeded rows will sometimes discourage crows from digging the seed as soon as your back is turned.

Unfortunately I am an "I hate to weed" gardener, and as this trait is hereditary, our offspring are nonweeders, too. Consequently our perennial and herb garden is crowded with old stalks, grasses and other irrelevant things. Come March, if the soil and moon are not right for planting potatoes and if primitive urges to garden are too strong for me to stay in by the fire, I ask my husband to sharpen the hoe and I head for the herb patch.

Perennial gardens need a sharp hoe during March.

Anise should be seeded.

Asparagus beds should be cut back and dressed with hardwood ashes and fertilizer.

Basil, wintered indoors, may be set out, or seeded in a sunny spot.

Bergamot and mint should be thinned and cut back.

Caraway planted in the fall should be thinned and fertilized.

Chives are set out in rich soil during March for summer pompoms.

Dill may be thickly seeded in a hot, sunny place.

Horseradish roots should be divided and the stalks cut back.

Lavender may be set out and the roots divided.

Parsley may be brought from the house and transplanted, or seeded in furrows.

Rhubarb should be fertilized and lightly cultivated. A little tobacco should be scattered to discourage grubs.

Rosemary should be lifted from its indoor wintering pot and replanted in gravel soil in a sunny spot.

Sage should be cut back for new growth.

Strawberries should be uncovered, runners cut and new plants set out.

Thyme should have mulch removed in March.

If there is any extra energy left after the herbs are set by for spring, berry bushes and winter onions should be cultivated, divided if they are too thick, and fertilized to force them for an early crop.

Herbs and perennial plants are peripheral fun but the nitty-gritty of gardening for our family is the kitchen garden (potatoes, tomatoes, beans and corn). Our kitchen garden is a half-acre south slope located a few hundred feet from our Culpeper County, Virginia, cabin.

Wild-food foraging starts in earnest in March. Uncle Steve regularly opened the season with a trip to the river for catties: catfish and cattails (*Typhaceae* family). First he consulted the almanac to see if the daily moon sign was congruent with the watery sign of Cancer, Pisces or Scorpio. The best days of the month to go fishing, he said, were those days ruled by a watery zodiac sign and the days on which the moon changed quarters. He emphasized that the day after the full moon was also excellent for catching fish. If all signals were favorable, he'd spade a fork of fishing worms from the coffee-ground-fed worm box, and off he'd go. If I was lucky and the appropriate day fell on a weekend or the Easter holidays, I'd go with him.

A side trip to the swamp for cattail roots was always in order before the "hard work" of catfishing began.

A marsh in March is a place of mystery and joy. Old bullrushes, rough as cats' tongues, rustle crankily before the wind. Browns and grays and frightening black holes transport the senses backward in time to the prehistoric mating of land and sea. Swamps are primitive regions. To wade in mud, half afraid, unseen life-forms lapping, merging with the leaden light of a blustery March morning, is eerie magic. To smell the swamp gasses as they reach for the atmosphere seeking intercourse with the sun is heady madness. Suddenly a duck, weighing man's threat against stiff, cold bones, bursts skyward and drops on another spot of the unfinished land.

Scratching for cattail roots in a swamp is a messy, frigid experience, but well worth the muck and cold. Carrying the same spading fork with which he had dug worms, my grandfather waded into the swamp, keeping to the hummocks as much as possible. I followed with a gunnysack as close as I could, remembering the horrible stories of quicksand. As I jumped from hummock to hummock, I repeatedly rehearsed where I would throw myself if I began to sink.

When a grouping of frowzy-looking cattail heads was selected, my grandfather would feel for the main roots with his fork. He said the clue to digging cattail roots was finding plants that grew in water because there the rootstock was often as large as a man's forearm, perpendicular and strongly anchored by fibrous rootlets. He said it was like pulling a cat's tooth to try to dig cattails in dry land.

He separated the surface of entanglements by hand, then followed the larger ropes to their knobby ends and removed the blunt sprouts. Sometimes he drew out handfuls of stringy fibers with bulbous ends and I would help him snap off the cattail tubers.

The main root is usually buried eight to ten inches deep in the muck, and my grandfather often reached down and cut off one end of the major root. This lump is somewhat bigger and softer than the tuberous root sprouts and is called the gasket. Although a gucky job, cattailing took only a few minutes because the roots were abundant and easy to snap, swish

45

clean in the swamp water and poke into the sack.

Before we left the marsh, Grandaddy let me pull a few cat-o'-nine-tail torches. Later, on a warm spring night, when the neighborhood kids and I would play Hide and Seek, I was allowed to dip a torch in coal oil and, after sticking it into the ground, light it. Weird shadows enhanced our play as we raced in and out of the smoky light with aboriginal abandon.

Catfish are positive thinkers; they might even be classified as impulse buyers. In March, after the air is warmed by the sun, catfish will take any bait, living or dead, but on a cold day, catfish are like coy women and need plenty of time to swallow the hook.

As long as it is strong, anything goes in the way of tackle for whisker fish, because when they strike, they head for the bottom. Some people try to return to the womb when wounded; a dog I knew would burrow into a haystack when its feelings were hurt; catfish head for hollow logs or undercut banks.

Catfish caught in cold water are particularly firm and good to eat. When their dense, sweet meat is skinned properly, no taint of mud remains. The ordinary catfish may be skinned readily by first immersing the cleaned fish into boiling water for one minute, then cutting off the head and dorsal fin, and peeling the skin back to the tail like a glove. The skin is cut away but the tail is left intact to facilitate handling. The fish is rolled in cornmeal and fried in deep fat until the flesh is tender and the outside golden.

Bulbous tubers from the shoots of cattail roots may be peeled and boiled in salted water for ten to twenty minutes, then served drenched in butter, salt and pepper. With crisp-fried fish, they are terrific!

The gaskets, or pulpy connecting joints of cattail rootstocks, cooked after being peeled, were used in stews by my family. I remember the taste as being reminiscent of parsnips.

Most root plants are better-tasting in the early spring because frosts seem to sweeten and tenderize them. But roots, if not marked, are difficult to identify. It is important to plan ahead and mark specific plants. It is important to study wild plants in all phases of their growth so that no error is made. I remember the Dare family once blew up like bloated frogs from eating iris roots which they said were mixed with cattail bases.

Candied sweet-flag roots! Even the name conjures up delightful memories. Sweet-flag root (*Acorus calamus*) has been used as a confection since the earliest recorded time. Flag-root candy is still made in northeastern communities that perpetuate pioneer ways of living.

Sweet-flag leaves resemble those of the poisonous iris plant, but when the blades of sweet flag are pinched they emit a gingerlike fragrance. Their flower is a light green spike that juts from one side of a leaf stalk like an ear of corn. The root is horizontal, about five inches below the mud, and it is usually topped with old leaves. Sweet-flag plants are found along the margins of ponds from Canada to Texas.

As children, we used to tug at roots any time of the year, pull back the brown outer layer and nibble on the fresh root. When raw, sweet flag is slippery and bites the tongue. Care should be taken to pinch and smell the tubers or leaves; sweet flag gives off a spicy fragrance. Blue flag, its poisonous cousin, is odorless and violently disagreeable in flavor.

Sweet-flag root, to be candied, must be peeled, chunked and simmered for several days until somewhat transparent. Lively smells will permeate the neighborhood and people will come to visit, hoping to taste the spiciness they smell. This is good. Because when they see the pallid squares their interest wanes and they leave the goodies behind. When the boiled roots are softish rather than hardish, sometimes as much as three days later, drain and measure. Cool and, using an equal amount of sugar and root bulk with about one-quarter cup of water to moisten, boil again. In the final boiling, which should be in a heavy pot, stir often until the sugar is almost absorbed and the roots take on a glossy topaz color. Remove the pot from the heat and quickly spoon the candied root onto wax paper and separate it into bite-sized pieces. Some people roll their candied root in granulated sugar but I find myself with not enough hands when it is time to separate the sweet flag before it hardens.

One last root for March: *Dioscorea.*

For several years I had been tantalized by a particularly attractive vine with picturesque seed pods shaped like bishops' hats that grows beside our cabin. Neither the local people nor their literature could identify my mystery plant, so I wrote to the National Arboretum, Department of Agriculture (a takeoff on my husband's philosophy: When all else fails, read the directions). Great! The Department of Agriculture wrote back saying that I had a species of wild yam. Beautiful! Everywhere I looked, wild yams! A new food source for starving humanity! I'd be rich! Savior of the Universe! Darwin, Burbank, Carver, Firth!

With deliberate speed and armed with buckets and shovels, Lewis and I attacked a male *Dioscorea.* I was determined to be discriminate with my new find because there are both males and mother plants, and I am all for motherhood. With relatively simple digging, we unearthed several male prizes. Big and beautiful! Hurrying home, I scrubbed our booty, removed its multitudinous rootlets, and, mouth watering, dropped them into boiling water.

Three days later they were still boiling, only in progressively smaller pots. Like the shrunken heads of the Orinoco my yams grew smaller and smaller.

Before they disappeared completely I rescued them, and they now grace my mantle. Gnarled and wizened, tough and tasteless, the primitive *Dioscorea* can be recommended only as a curio.

Early greens are, I believe, the most popular and widely appreciated wild food. Basically, potherbs fall into two types. First are those that may be picked, washed and put into a little boiling water with a pinch of salt, boiled briefly, and served with butter or bacon drippings. The second type is endowed with a strong flavor and must be cooked in two or more waters to extract the bitterness, then treated as the mild greens with butter or drippings.

Mildness is a relative term, and to some people my tender, sweet greens might be classified as strong and tough. In that case, I would suggest boiling them and throwing off several waters before flavoring.

March greens to be boiled briefly: dayflower, daylily, amaranth, shepherd's purse, mustard, winter-cress, watercress, and wild lettuce. These should be identified during the summer and marked for picking the following spring. Mix or match them.

Dayflower, Spiderwort family (*Commelina communis*). The succulent creeping stems support alternate short irislike leaves, and in the late summer two- or three-petaled blue flowers appear. *Commelina* is found on waste lots from New York and Minnesota southward, and it is often found growing rank along small streams. Tender young dayflower shoots have both a rich green flavor and color when boiled about five minutes in salted water. Our family prefers them well drained and served with a plop of butter. A neighbor sprinkles her dayflower greens with nutmeg.

Daylily (*Hemerocallis fulva*). The long swordlike leaves surround the base of leafless woody stems that bear orange lilies. Daylilies have escaped gardens to grow along roadsides and creek banks from Canada to Virginia. Shoots, cut when three to four inches high, are a favored early potherb; they are non-gritty and easy to gather, and their flavor, when boiled for four minutes in salted water, is mild and pleasant. I have found by experimenting that cutting early shoots does not harm the plant or inhibit flowering. The clue to excellent-tasting daylily sprouts is quick cooking and thorough draining. If they are allowed to boil too long they become slippery; also, daylilies tend to hold water, and should be shaken in the colander before serving.

Amaranth, or wild beet (*Amaranthus*). The coarse veiny leaves may discourage some people from picking this potherb —it really is an ugly plant. Amaranth has nothing going for it except its availability and taste. Its leaves are oval, somewhat pointed, and dense, elongate clusters of seedlike green flowers and bristles clutch the main stalks each August. The root is pink to red and tough to pull when the plant is old. This plant grows along roadsides and on wasteland from Canada southward.

I use the whole plant when the wild beet is four or five inches high, or I pluck tender leaves later in the season. They do not boil down as some greens do, and are not bright green when cooked, but for a sweet spinachlike potherb, amaranth is highly recommended. I especially like to mix it with the more highly colored greens such as lamb's-quarters later in the season.

Shepherd's purse (*Capsella bursa-pastoris*). A rosette of coarsely toothed leaves somewhat resembling a large dandelion plant forms the base for a single stem of clustered tiny white flowers. Seedpods are heart-shaped to form an inverted purse. Shepherd's purse is found throughout the northeastern and north central United States in gardens and along roads.

Although shepherd's purse resembles turnip or cabbage in taste, it is considerably milder than either. Each spring I walk over the lawn and twist out the new center foliage, which is easy to spot because it greens up earlier than grass. Shepherd's purse must be washed in several waters before cooking because the rosettes catch grit.

Winter-cress, watercress, spring cress, and rocket need no introduction to most greens fanciers. Mildly mustardlike, they are bitey, hard-rock American, and great to eat in March.

Greens to be boiled in several waters until mild-flavored and tender, and actually best if served chopped, are: wild onions and leeks, chicory, dock, dandelion, salsify and skunk-cabbage. These also may be mixed or matched.

Wild onions (*Allium* family). Many suburban dwellers do not realize that the wild onions that push up through their dormant spring lawns cook into a sweet potherb. My family looks forward to a dish of wild onions, chopped, cooked until mild, then served smothered in cream sauce and drizzled over with thin slivers of cheese.

Wild leeks (*Allium tricoccum*). This flat-leafed weed found clustering in low areas may be boiled to make a delicious green. The whole plant, after removal of roots and dry outer leaves, is washed and plunged into boiling water. If after cooking for fifteen minutes the onionlike leek flavor is too strong, pour off the water and boil a second or third time. Serve wild leeks with butter or creamed, or chop for use in a delicate onion soup.

Wild onions and leeks, though relatives to the ramp and tough garlic, are surprisingly sweet and palatable.

Chicory (*Cichorium intybus*) and dandelion (*Taraxacum* family). Both of these familiar potherbs, with jagged leaves and milk-exuding stems, are found throughout the temperate areas of the United States and Canada. Chicory bears blue flowers on a rigid stem. Proclaimed as the best greens by some people, both plants are gathered with enthusiasm. After several thorough washings, dandelion and chicory rosettes and leaves should be plunged into boiling water to remove the herby taste. I prefer to further reduce the bitterness by repeated boilings. I change chicory water at least three times, then flavor the greens with chopped bacon and drippings in which a little onion has been sautéed.

Dock (*Rumex* family). The young leaves of dock boil into a soft, somewhat sour-flavored green. Most species of dock are palatable after several boilings, but a few remain bitter and strong-tasting. The most common species with narrow leaves are tender and edible all summer, but docks with veiny, round leaves soon become strong. Dock leaves do not hold their shape after cooking; rather, they become one mass of green. For that reason I usually mix them with other potherbs before serving them with butter or bacon drippings.

Salsify, oyster-plant or goat's-beard (*Tragopogon*). When immature, salsify rosettes made up of broad grass-blade leaves may be cut or twisted from the root with no difficulty. After the first year salsify grows one to three feet tall and develops pointed bracts that support yellow dandelion-type flowers. The young plants are the tenderest and sweetest. Found in waste lots from Canada southward, salsify resembles dandelion in flavor and is often picked and prepared with it.

I have heard of boiling young skunk-cabbage (*Symplocarpus foetidus*) but I have not dismembered the solitary plant that grows in our creek to try it. A lady told me that her family eats and enjoys "a mess of cabbage" each spring. She said that after it is cooked in three waters, to each of which a half-teaspoon of baking soda is added, the cabbage is rinsed in hot water, chopped, salted and served with sweetened vinegar and bacon-onion sauce similar to that used in wilted lettuce. She insisted that the malodorous smell of the raw plant does not permeate the cooked greens.

The leaves of skunk-cabbage all sprout from the root like a loosely knit head of domestic cabbage. There is no stem as such. The leaves are bright, moist green, rounded at the base and not folded. Caution must be taken to positively identify skunk-cabbage, because it resembles the toxic Indian poke or white hellebore (*Veratrum viride*). Indian poke is a violent poison.

Skunk-cabbage is found in marshes in Alaska and across the United States. The natives of Alaska eat the young leaves of skunk-cabbage. Moose love them. Dogs roll in them to cover their own scent. And bears are said to nibble them as a spring tonic and an ursus aphrodisiac.

Hunting wild spring greens is often a marrow-chilling, damp and disappointing adventure, but gathering a potful of tender herbs each March satisfies. Not only do early greens taste good, but by the very act of searching sunny slopes man renews his ties with the earth.

Our neighbors in Missouri used to home-can mild greens each spring. When preserving low-acid vegetables such as cress, extra processing or boiling time is needed to prevent spoilage. Wash, rinse, drain and chop any combination of mild greens. Cut off tough stems and cover with boiling water to wilt. Place the pan over a fire, turn the greens and, just as they begin to boil, pack them into hot, sterilized quart jars. Cut through the greens several times with a sharp knife, add a teaspoon of salt and a tablespoon of vinegar to each quart, and fill the jar to within one inch of the top with boiling water. Wipe each jar lip, screw down the lids and process jars three hours in a boiling-water bath. When the jars are removed from the canner, cool them slowly.

Moon-sign followers believe that canning and preserving are best done under dry zodiac signs and they can wild greens under Aries and Gemini.

Native Alaskans rarely preserve greens for winter but I tasted one family's sauerkraut made of Eskimo rhubarb (*Polygonum alaskanum*), sweet coltsfoot (*Petasites frigidus*), and purslane (*Arenaria peploides*). They explained how they had brined the mature leaves in salt, and I found that their method was similar to my cabbage kraut techniques. Although less crisp, their brined greens were tasty and enlivened our meal of roast reindeer.

Preserving the gifts of the earth has long been man's self-mandated obligation. Nearly all peoples have devised ways of preserving surplus food. Saving is a mark of maturation. People who live close to the soil say that saving starts with the first green of March.

IV
Mountains of Herring and Hen Fruit with Oceans of Oysters and Greens
APRIL

Moon lore of Aries. Gardening by the moon, temperatures and time. Wild potherbs: pepper-grass, pennycress, mustard. Oysters, keeping in bushel, oysters and new greens, Eskimo oysters, oyster frills, pickled oysters. Herring: deviled, stewed, marinated, pickled, in sour cream. Smoking fish, hot and cold methods. Native smoked herring. Eggs preserved in wax and salted. Eskimos and eggs. April and eggs as symbols of hope.

APRIL IS BEST for grubbing. When the moon is in the barren sign of Aries (March 21 to April 20) noxious weeds and unwanted growth may be destroyed. It is also best to turn sod or to plant posts during the barren Aries reign, especially during the last quarter of the moon or the first three days of the new moon.

After I graduated from high school in Maysville, Missouri, and did a hitch in the Teacher's College, I accepted a position as teacher at White Dove School # 49, DeKalb County. I boarded at a farm with featherbeds, a magnificent pine tree that moaned in the wind, and a gander who chased me halfway to school each day. Mr. and Mrs. Halman, the good farm couple with whom I stayed, worked their garden by the moon. During the first twenty days of April they weeded, thinned herbs and prepared the soil. They believed that plants sown under the sign of Aries would grow rank and full-leafed but would wither before producing food. Aries, they said, ruled with a fiery, dry, barren and masculine hand. Aries plantings would grow quickly, but would hold no fruit; they would fool gardeners with their fancy growth but the plant development would be of short duration.

Mr. Halman knew more about moon signs and zodiac lore for farming than any one I've ever known. He didn't come in to breakfast until he had studied the signs. Actually, he had all kinds of zodiac information in the outhouse. The Halmans didn't use toilet paper or Sears Roebuck catalogs—they had a stack of old almanacs. After the current Virgo page was missing in September and Mr. Halman sulked, Mrs. Halman drew me aside and instructed me always to take from the bottom of the pile, because the new almanac was for reading.

57

Mr. Halman believed that if a man was to be successful and content he must work in harmony with nature. "Put your work in time with her vibrations," he often told me.

Although my grandfather had an early garden, a Pisces planting, Mr. Halman did not plow his garden until the sign of Aries (barren, thus discouraging weed-seed growth), and he waited until Taurus (April 20 to May 21) to plant his main garden as well as his farm crops. Taurus, the bull, was said to be an earthy, moist and productive zodiac sign, and a fruitful constellation under which to plant. The Taurus moon is hearty, Mr. Halman said, and growing things respond with vigor if seeded at that time. He would wax poetic about the virtues of "the bull." Strength from its earthy influence, yet characterized by feminine productivity, he would claim.

Mr. Halman also seriously considered the moon phase in all his farming endeavors. During the first quarter of the moon under Taurus he planted broccoli, barley, cabbage, corn, lettuce, chard, kale, endive, oats, rye, spinach and other leafy vegetables.

During the second quarter of the moon under Taurus he planted beans, peas, squash and tomatoes.

In the third quarter he planted beets, carrots, parsnips, potatoes, radishes, rutabagas, turnips, onions and bulbous flowering plants.

The fourth quarter was a bad sign for seeding, Mr. Halman declared, so he would mow, prepare soil, cut in the wood lot, fix fences and work around the barn.

There was one planting chore about which both Mr. Halman and my grandfather were in emphatic agreement: they planted corn when apple trees were in bloom.

They also agreed that temperatures should be watched because temperature determines harvest time. If daytime temperatures were 75° F. or above, they believed that beans, beets, chard, cucumbers, kale, lettuce, okra, onions, peas, spinach and summer squash would be ready to harvest in from six to eight weeks after planting. With temperatures in the 80s, sweet corn, limas, carrots, potatoes and melons usually ripen in ten to twelve weeks.

April gardens are often faceless squares of soil, thus foraging greens in April before gardens came in was an accepted way of life during the Depression in Missouri. Seeing people systematically searching fields for edible greens always reminds me of Millet's "The Gleaners." There is something peaceful about witnessing a family working together toward a common goal, and during the 1930s, simply feeding a family was an important goal to many.

I think my White Dove days were where I really learned to appreciate greens. A mixture of boiled and drained greens, sprinkled with crisp fried bacon chopped with tidbits of onion, is hard to beat. Mrs. Halman always immersed her greens in boiling water rather than cold water, because she said it cut the herby taste. If the greens were strong-tasting she would sometimes boil them in a second water.

Mrs. Halman's spring greens with gravy were something else. She would cook, drain and chop a variety of early potherbs and in a skillet fry crumbled country sausage until well done, then drain off a part of the grease. Into the sausage and drippings she would put two tablespoons of flour, a little salt, pepper; swing it all around with a fork, and when it was starting to brown, add about a cup and a half of milk, stirring constantly. She let it boil and thicken about three minutes while she spooned the cooked, chopped greens into individual sauce dishes and topped them with a dab of butter. Just as we were sitting at the table, she'd stir a cup of sour cream into the sausage gravy and pour it over the greens. Robust, spicy and delicious.

Many of the wild potherbs gathered in April belong to the mustard family, *Cruciferae*, so called because their flower petals form a cross. The mustard cousins, *Brassica*, together with vigorous young shoots of pepper-grass (*Lepidium*), horse-radish (*Armoracia lapathifolia*), pennycress (*Thlaspi arvense*), sea-rocket (*Cakile edentula*), scurvy grass (*Cochlearia*) and other cress greens, make palatable and zesty vegetables. I like most of these greens cooked in two or more waters, then flavored with butter or drippings. They all have a turnipy-horse-radishy flavor, and if this is offensive they should be combined with mild greens such as young amaranth (*Amaranthus*), Japanese knotweed (*Polygonum cuspidatum*), or dayflowers (*Commelina communis*).

All potherbs should be used when the shoots are very young, and practically any of them may be cooked, then served cold as a salad. My grandmother often cooked a double batch so she could flavor the leftovers with oil, vinegar and a little sugar, salt, pepper and sometimes a bit of onion.

When wild greens were at their height each April, Mrs. Halman was mysteriously attacked by a craving for oysters. She began to whet her appetite by describing to me the delicate fragrance and succulence of oysters when cooked with greens. A day or two later she mentioned to her husband that it was April, the last month with *R* until September. I had heard people say that oysters should be taken only during the months with R in their spelling, so I understood the overtones.

A week later Mrs. Halman became quite emphatic and announced that if her husband wasn't going to Kansas City, where they purchased live oysters by the bushel, she was going to crank the Ford and drive the hundred miles herself. If there was one thing Mr. Halman liked better than his wife, it was his car; although it was seven years old, he treated it like a new mistress. The thought of his wife herding his mistress down the road was apparently too much. The following morning I heard Mr. Halman declare that he was going to K.C., and Mrs. H. grinned as she cautioned him about making sure that the oysters were unwashed and that they had lots of seaweed around them. "Gotta feed themselves for a month or more," she told me as we waved her husband off to the fish market.

APRIL

When Mr. Halman returned late that night, both Halmans worked together covering the baskets of the biggest oysters with chopped ice sprinkled with cornmeal, wet newspapers and gunnysacks. They then tucked their hoard into the vegetable cave. The rest of the oysters were for eating now they said, as they called me to join them.

Mr. Halman had been drinking a little and he was very happy. He lit a lantern and went out and sat on the stones near the pump and started shucking oysters and eating them. Mrs. Halman brought out some spicy sauce and crackers, and the three of us sat by the well devouring raw oysters by lantern light.

They both had their fill of oysters every year, they told me; even during hard times they always saved a calf to trade for April oysters.

The bushels they kept in the fruit cellar had to have new ice and cornmeal every week or so, and the last oysters I had in May just before I left were almost as tasty as the half-bushel we killed on the rock that first night.

Mrs. Halman's primary reason for wanting oysters in the spring was so that she could cook oysters and new greens.

Pick about two quarts of mild greens such as dayflower shoots, amaranth tips, cress, lamb's-quarters and a few sorrel plants, wash, boil briefly (about four minutes) in salted water, drain and chop finely. Mince a handful of wild-onion tops and fry lightly in butter. Add the chopped, cooked greens, a small clump of chopped parsley, two tablespoons of oyster liquor, two tablespoons of cream and a bouillon cube dissolved in two tablespoons of the boiling greens liquid to the sautéed onion in the skillet. Season the greens with salt, pepper and a little nutmeg, spoon into a buttered casserole and dot with butter. Save about three tablespoons of greens for topping. Cover the casserole with a pint of raw oysters, and spoon the remaining greens around the oysters but do not cover them completely. Sprinkle the top with bread crumbs, dots of butter, pepper, salt, and pop into a brisk oven for about seven minutes. When the oysters become puffy and their edges curl, serve at once with crackling bread.

I had oysters and new greens three times that spring and I always meant to go back another April because it is doubtful that God and Mrs. Halman ever produced a more satisfying food.

Mrs. Halman also fixed Eskimo oysters: a raw oyster tucked into a patty of mashed potatoes and fried brown in butter.

Her oyster frills for breakfast consisted of a pint of oysters turned into a piping-hot skillet, and seasoned with salt and pepper. When their edges frilled, a tablespoon of butter was added and the whole pan was poured immediately over hot buttered toast.

Boxed oysters, gumbo, toddle: Mrs. Halman served them all. Then, before the season was over, she pickled some. Heat a quart of oysters in their own liquid until plump. Drain, save the juice, and add one-half cup of malt vinegar, one teaspoon salt, eight cloves, eight peppercorns, two blades of mace and one hot red pepper pod to the oyster liquor. Simmer five minutes, skim, pour over the oysters, cool overnight and eat the next day or seal in sterilized pint jars.

Mrs. Halman stored the pickled oysters three or four weeks in the cave but she said she didn't really know how long they would keep because Mr. H. would sneak down and eat a pint whenever he was oyster-hungry. Quite frankly I prefer my oysters raw or cooked and have never felt oyster-rich enough to risk pickling any.

Sāk, an Indian name meaning "Month When Herring Are Eaten," traditionally marks the end of northland famine fears. Although herring often begin to run in March, April is the time many families "put down" the blue-and-silver fish into pickle, brine, smoke, wine or sour-cream sauce.

Strangely, I do not remember herring in Connecticut, but herring behind the kitchen door in Missouri I do remember.

I remember, too, slicing heaps of onions for pickling herring, feeling sorry for myself, yet enjoying my tears.

Each April my grandparents bought a barrel of salt herring, which they pickled in the kitchen. For a week or so before they started pickling the fish, we ate grilled herring, marinated herring, stewed herring and herring deviled in mustard. The bones of salted herring do not seem to be as prominent as in fresh fish so the preparation and eating of herring dishes was simplified.

First, the fish were leached of salt by soaking in cold water or in skimmed milk overnight, then drained, cleaned, rinsed, trimmed and towel-dried.

For deviling we slit the prepared herring from the backbone and ribs, coated each side with mustard, sprinkled them with bread crumbs, butter, pepper and salt (if needed), and we broiled the nearly boneless fish halves for seven minutes on each side, or until done.

For stewed herring we chunked six leached and prepared fish into an enamel pot, dotted them with butter, pepper and salt (if needed), tossed in one cup of dry white wine and brought everything to a boil. Then the flame was lowered, the pot covered, and the contents simmered for fifteen minutes. We removed the herring from the pot and boiled the liquid down by half. We arranged the fish in a shallow bowl, sprinkled them with small pieces of butter, and poured the hot, reduced liquid over them. Served with a bland casserole such as scalloped potatoes, a side dish of spinach, and lemon-meringue pie, a supper of stewed herring in the spring awakens dormant taste buds.

I have marinated leached salt herring and served it cold as a relish or as a main dish. Marinated herring will keep in the refrigerator one or two weeks.

For marinating three or four medium-sized herring, I soak, drain, clean, rinse, trim and dry each fish. If they are large, I cut them into manageable-size pieces; then I put them with a layer of sliced onions and thinly sliced carrots into an enamel kettle and add one-half cup of white wine and one-half cup of white vinegar. I sprinkle on a pinch of thyme and parsley, a bay leaf, six peppercorns and six cloves. I cut a circle of wax paper and put it over the fish to retain the moisture. The whole dish is brought to a boil, and when the liquid shows bubbles below the paper I lower the fire, cover the pan and simmer it for fifteen minutes. I let the fish cool in the marinade, remove the wax paper and serve. Actually marinated herring are more tasty if allowed to stand in the refrigerator for at least twenty-four hours before serving.

Pickling herring each spring is a ritual in some societies. In my opinion the lack of meaningful ritual in our modern world contributes to the rootless feelings of many people. To be sure, there are perennial TV shows, the yellow school bus, sock hops, fire sirens and sports seasons, but ritual that relates to the natural order of life seems minimized.

Pickling herring is quite simple. The first consideration is the type of herring used. In addition to fresh herring (which if used for pickling must be salted at least six hours to firm the fish), four main types of herring are sold by fish merchants.

1. Pickled herring—which are really only preserved in brine.

2. The New York schmaltz—younger, fatter fish with less salt preservative.

3. Mathes or matjes—preserved in sugar, salt, vinegar and spices.

4. Salt herring—put down in barrels with alternate layers of dry salt.

Depending upon the method of preservation, the herring must be soaked in water from four hours to six days in order to leach the salt from them. Some people do not soak matjes at all.

For pickling large quantities of schmaltz, my grandmother

used to soak the fish overnight in ice water in the icebox. "Winegar mills," or milch pickles, were her mainstay. After soaking to leach the salt, she cleaned, beheaded, skinned and filleted each herring, being careful to save the milch, or male secretion, but not worrying about small bones because these seem to disappear in pickling. The large bones were cut away. The fish were rinsed in cold water.

For every fifteen herrings she made a mix of two cups of white vinegar, four-and-a-half cups of water, two tablespoons of pickling spices, one cup of sugar, and salt if needed. She tasted the leached fish to test their saltiness. She boiled the pickling mixture for fifteen minutes. While it cooled, the fillets were dried on cloth towels and six large Spanish onions were sliced. The milch that she had collected was pressed through a sieve to remove membranes, and it was stirred into the cooled vinegar mixture.

Into a two-and-a-half-gallon crock behind the kitchen door she laid alternate layers of herring and onions. She put the bigger chunks of fish on the bottom and the smaller ones on the top because they pickle faster and could be eaten sooner. When the crock was nearly filled with fish she poured the "winegar mills" over it, shook the crock to settle the ingredients, then covered it with a dinner plate, a rock and a cloth. The herring at the top were ready to eat in a week. As soon as we had a few messes, or when the weather became warm, Grandaddy moved the crocks to the fruit cellar, where the temperature remained cool.

Grandma's pickled herring kept for three months and became tastier every day but grew less firm the longer we kept them after six weeks.

Some years, when we had lots of milk, we would eat Winegar Mills in Sour Cream. We drained five or six of the pickled herring and combined them with their pickled onions in a pint or so of sour cream. These were very rich, and eating too many just before going to bed would create grandiose dreams.

The LSD fantasies I have read can't compare with the multi-colored dreams I had after eating a pint of pickled herring in sour cream at bedtime.

In recent years I have pickled fresh herring by salting them first and using Grandma's recipe, but omitting the milch. I have used wine vinegar instead of white, and the ruby fish and onion slices are beautiful.

Fresh fish to be smoked should be salted or soaked in brine first in order to firm the meat and discourage bacteria growth. The salinity of the brine depends upon the size of the fish and the length of time a person wants to preserve them. I knew a convivial cook at a boarding school in Alaska who brined 100 percent. That is, straight salt was rubbed into the meat, and she kept the fish in brine for eight days before smoking. She said her smoked fish would keep forever, but as her husband asked, who wants to keep fish forever?

Some people brine their fresh herring in half-and-half salt and water for twenty-four to forty-eight hours before smoking them.

When I questioned one friend about the amount of salt required to make a brine, he said, "If a potato with an eight-penny nail in her will float, she's salty."

Another smoking cohort soaks the cleaned fish for three hours in brine that floats an unopened can of evaporated milk.

I usually scale, clean and cut off the head of fresh herring, then slice the fish lengthwise along one side of the backbone to the tail, which is left on to keep the entire fish in a single piece. The tail connection facilitates hanging the herring over the smoke rack. I then immerse the fish in a potato-floating brine for three hours while I get the fire going. As in pickling fish, I remove the larger bones, but the small bones are no bother after the herring have been smoked.

In Alaska I used alder wood for smoking, but any non-resinous hardwood works fine. Hickory, beech or oak are tra-ditional. Green wood, of course, gives the best smoke; some people use spicebush or juniper berries for fragrance, but I can't tell the difference.

Home smoking chambers do not have to be elaborate. I have used boxes with piano wire strung across from side to side; a teepee of poles covered with green leaves and a tarp; and once I used a dynamiter's shack.

I always work with small quantities of fish when I smoke, usually a washtubful, as the fish must hang freely and my smokehouses are always small.

There are two methods of smoking fish: hot-smoke and cold. In cold-smoke the fish are hung away from the fire and smoked at a temperature of around 90° F. Hot-smoke means that the fish are partially cooked and dried in the process by being hung close to the fire.

The hardest work I have found in cold-smoking fish is digging the hole. For my backyard operation, I dig a fire pit about two feet deep and three feet across. On one side of the pit, beginning about ten inches down, I dig a trench about eight inches wide, which leads from the fire pit approximately three feet to exit into the smoking chamber. This trench carries the smoke from the fire to the fish and should be gradually inclined toward the surface of the ground.

My smoking chambers are always mobile, so I can easily pull the box away while the fire is getting started. I allow the fire to burn down, then load on green wood, chips or sawdust to create a smudge. When the fire is established and smoking well, I cover the fire pit with a piece of sheet metal and the trench with a plank. I leave an opening to the windward side of the pit opposite the trench side so that the fire can draw and so I can stoke it without removing the cover. I also dig out a sort of mouth or apron opening to the fire pit to make stoking easier.

When smoke is pouring from the distant end of the trench, I tilt the smoke chamber and fling the herring across the zig-zag wires, tails up. I then move the box back over the smoking trench opening and cold-smoke.

The box, which weeps smoke from its upper cracks, should be waterproof on the top because it always rains at night when you have to get up and stoke. If there is as much rain as in Sitka, Alaska, a small run-off trench should be dug around the fire pit; otherwise you will wake up some night with a floating fire.

In three or four days, when the fish are dried but not quite mummified, I lay them out in the house to cure for a week, nibbling at intervals to see if they are good, and then I wrap them in brown paper and store them in the icebox. Cold-smoked herring do not keep indefinitely without refrigeration, and I do not smoke this type with the idea of preserving for winter use.

Some people hot-smoke. For this method, a more permanent arrangement is needed because the fire is built in the smoking chamber. Hot-smoking has to be watched more carefully so that the fish will not barbecue. The temperature must be raised slowly to 140° F. If the fish appear to be cooking, lower the temperature by putting wet sawdust on the fire. In a real smokehouse you can control the heat by hoisting the fish up the chimney or opening a vent. It takes two to four hours of hot smoke to flavor most fish.

If skin is left on the fish during smoking, it is advisable to hang them skin side out so that the moist, glazed meat will not become black and hardened.

The man who drills his potato with a nail to measure salinity cans both types of smoked fish by putting chunks of smoked fish into sterilized jars and sealing them with heat. Other people take their smoked herring to commercial canners. If smoked fish are expected to keep a long time, they must initially be salted heavily and smoked until they are jerky dry.

Native Alaskans do not rely on herring oil as they once had to do. They used to brine and smoke, then preserve their fish in oil, afterwards using the herring oil in cooking. Today, like everyone else, they buy butter, salad oil and hand lotions.

Some native Alaskans utilize modern, and often communal, smokehouses for their herring, but on a bright day it is still not unusual to pass villages and see racks of drying fish, brine barrels and smoke fires. Most native-prepared fish are brined, sun-dried for three or four days and smoked two weeks or so. The weather, the type of fish, the time of year, and tribal customs vary; but I love to eat "squaw candy," as Alaskans call smoked fish. To my taste, no fancy store-bought fish can rival the chewy native varieties.

Eggs and April go together.

In Missouri, Grandma always kept a few hens, and when we had a surplus of eggs she put down some for cooking. She packed them in dry salt, small end down, and kept the egg keg in a cool place but where the eggs would not freeze. As an added precaution she sometimes rubbed lard into the eggshells and poured melted lard (130° F.) upon the topmost layer of salt.

For plain waxed eggs, which were better for eating than salted ones, she heated a pan of water, melted a square of paraffin in it and then cooled the water to about 120° F. Each fresh, room-temperature egg was candled to be sure that it was not fertile, then, held delicately with tongs, it was quickly dipped in and out of the floating paraffin. I liked to help dip. I worked with six eggs, one at a time, and laid them on a paper after the quick immersion in the paraffin. I moved the water and wax to the front of the cook stove to keep it warm while I cradled each egg.

Cradling is a sensuously satisfying exercise. Take the first egg dipped and press it between both palms. Turn and press it, turn and press it, continuing to rub the warm egg with the palms until the surface feels smooth and waxy. The coating of paraffin should not be thick enough to pull off, but rather to serve as a seal. The clue to success in waxing eggs is to use fresh eggs at room temperature and work fast.

My grandmother laid each waxed egg on a bed of clean

straw in a barrel with all layers of eggs separated by fresh straw. The keg was covered with straw and secured with a lid before being stored in the coolest, darkest corner of the vegetable-root cellar.

Grandma's cooking eggs and waxed eggs lasted throughout the following winter, and although she always broke each preserved egg into a small bowl before using, I do not remember a spoiled egg.

Native peoples along the lower Kuskokwim in Alaska have long used seal oil and other fats to preserve duck eggs for winter. Traditionally they used the stomach of a seal, which had been scraped and dried, and after securing one end, they filled it with unbroken eggs and seal oil. Those Eskimos were not overly careful about selecting infertile eggs because they relished the rich embryo, nor were they particular about eggshells. They believed that eating any eggshell was "to cut your mother-in-law." One banty-rooster-type Eskimo I knew devoured eggshells by the mouthful. Crunching, eyes glittering, he chewed shells even as he was dying of tuberculosis. His fat mother-in-law would come to visit him in the sanatorium and she would sit like a sleepy frog with a gloating grin on her face. She didn't like him, either. The last I heard she was still going strong, but the little Eskimo had long since done his part to increase the lime content of a little plot of land above the river.

Bladderfuls of eggs were often brought as part of a male dowry when a young swain went to visit the family of his chosen mate. Eggs were symbolic of life to the tundra Eskimos.

The egg is still a symbol of new life in many societies. April, with its new gardens, greens and eggs, is symbolic of new life, too. April is a time of hope.

V

The Earth Blooms
MAY

Moon in Taurus and garden tools. Transplanting seedlings, seeding leafy "neck vegetables": chard, endive, lettuce, spinach. Plant melons, cucumbers, pole beans, limas and corn. Potatoes, carrots, beets and peanuts by the dark of Taurus. Cultivate during fourth quarter. Stagger plantings. Wild foods: strawberries, morel mushrooms, and sprouts of poke, milkweed, asparagus and bracken. Flower wines: daisy, honeysuckle, rose. Roses: in tea, preserving, pickled buds. Sachets, insect deterrents, rose jar. Bees, honey remedies, mead with blossoms and pineapple. May brings warmth.

THE MONTH OF MAY is one of the most pleasant times to garden, and the proper tools make the task lighter. Tools need not be fancy or numerous, but they must fit the job. A practical list might include: wheelbarrow, garden cultivator or rotary tiller (personally, a tiller makes me feel as if I'm on the business end of a jack-hammer, so I use the old push-pull cultivator), rake, field hoe, trowel and a long-handled, pointed shovel.

Some people include a spading fork, a leaf rake or a flat Dutch hoe. A string to stretch between the sides of the garden to help make the rows straight, a couple of cheap buckets and an old knife are handy, too.

In early May, while the zodiac sign is in the earthy, moist, productive, feminine sign of Taurus (April 20 to May 21), planting is the main chore. Moon-sign followers would say to avoid the first day of the new moon, but during the first quarter my grandfather transplanted broccoli, Brussels sprouts, cabbage and cauliflower, and he planted Swiss chard, sweet corn, endive, lettuce and spinach. Taurus rules the neck, he said, and leafy "neck vegetables" should be planted on the waxing Taurus moon. During the second quarter of the moon under Taurus, astrologers advocate replanting snap beans and summer squash; and planting melons, late squash, cucumbers, pole beans, black-eyed peas, limas and okra. Tomatoes, eggplant, peppers and celery should be set out during the second quarter of the moon.

Corn is traditionally planted on the waxing moons from apple-blossom time until the fourth of July. Some moon-sign followers call corn a "neck vegetable," others call it "stem fruit." They advocate that "stem fruit" is best planted during the second quarter of the moon.

After the moon is full, Taurus is particularly favorable for the planting of potatoes, carrots, beets, turnips, sweet potatoes, salsify, onions and peanuts.

Fertilize, side-dress with sawdust, compost or mulch, thin and cultivate during the fourth quarter of the moon.

The zodiac sign changes on May 21 when Gemini takes over with his twin characteristics: dryness and barrenness. If you garden by the moon's signs, you should destroy unwanted growing things, trim, weed and cut timber and fence posts under the sign of Gemini. My grandfather would say to cultivate under Gemini (May 21 to June 21).

Destroying weed seedlings under the Twins give twin benefits of timing and rhythm, moon-sign followers believe. They say that living things on earth constantly swing between life and death. Timing to destroy or harvest is just as important as timing to nurture life. Rhythm is as important in death as it is in life, one moon lady told me, and she emphasized that the Twins rule the arms, or the manifestation of timing and rhythm.

If peas ripen during Gemini's reign, they should be harvested and canned or dried because they will keep well, astrologers predict. If kale ripens, it should be cut and canned.

In order to have fresh produce over a longer period, I usually stagger some of my plantings. For example, I drop in four or five plantings of green beans. Thus, if the sign is wrong, or the varmints are hungry, or if it is too dry or hot, by the odds, one of the plantings will make.

Sometimes I buy different varieties for each planting. I like yellow wax, purple pod and stringless green bush beans. In addition to bush, I sow pole and lima beans, so we can have fresh beans from June until October.

Endive, kale, chard and spinach may also be alternated in staggered plantings from March to May.

Lettuce is fun to grow because it comes up on time, is distinctive in appearance and has the decency to die before everyone is tired of it. Lettuce may be staggered in plantings until the weather is hot, then sowed again in early fall.

To insure continuous fruiting, a pinch of cucumbers may be planted at intervals around a main planting for use as pickles.

Muskmelons take about three months to ripen and are difficult to grow, so they should be started at one time. The plants are beautiful. The time we grew softball-sized melons, we measured and thumped and waited patiently. Obviously the Culpeper County Chapter of the Virginia Association of Terrapins was thumping and waiting, too, because when we picked them they were cleaned out. The garden was full of muskmelon rinds. The little sneak thieves had eaten the insides of our melons without removing them from the vines.

With flowers like hollyhocks, pods that give you the itch, and a taste reminiscent of oysters when fried, okra are classic schizophrenic plants. When they are old, they are horrid. I knew a man who was so in love with okra he was going to form an okra co-op in Kansas and populate the state with okra eaters. For most of us, one planting should produce all the okra a family needs.

Onion sets should be started early in the season with staggered plantings in May, August and October. Such exotic varieties as big reds and bunched whites are fun. Green onions are passion food to some people. We have a friend, executive type, who comes to visit us in the country just so he can pull some onions, then sit on the back porch with us and eat them with Limburger cheese, drink beer and talk. We have some wild and malodorous discussions.

If a person is strictly the nongreen-thumb type, and suffers insecurity from his affliction, all is not lost. Plant squash. Squash will grow nearly anywhere for anyone in May. Summer yellows multiply prolifically; zucchini grow like baseball bats, though they are best eaten as six-inch virgins; mealy winter squash grow rampantly at the drop of a seed.

From May through July, summer squash may be staggered to insure young fruit all season.

Many plantings of watermelon can produce vigorous vines, but response is often spotty because watermelons take about four months to mature and lots can happen in that time. Crows dig up seeds, hail knocks down plants, and cutworms cut.

Gardening is fun. Work? Yes. But with a vegetable garden there is always hope. There is hope in old friendly vegetable varieties and in new types; unusual vegetables add zest to the commonplace, so it is good to try one far-out crop each year. It is also desirable to know what you're trying. We planted black salsify one time, and we didn't know we were supposed to eat the roots. Black salsify greens are terrible.

Strawberries are another matter; everyone knows what part to eat. In my mind's calendar, May 31, Memorial Day, is time to go strawberry picking. Of course, in Florida the plump berries start producing in February, and in Alaska, Fourth of July is the time to take a boat to Strawberry Point near Juneau and wallow in the native tradition of strawberries and love.

Throughout the middle states, May–June means strawberry shortcake, pie, jam, ice cream and wine. Wild strawberries (*Fragaria virginiana*), while no larger than a fingernail, hold a flavor vastly superior to most cultivated varieties but are far more fragile. Great care must be taken to pick berries without grit, sticks or buttercups, because the mushy consistency of wild strawberries does not favor washing. South slopes of open fields are likely spots to forage because the plants must emerge, bloom and bear before high weeds obscure the sun.

One year our strawberry hill had been white with blossoms, so that when Aunt Ellen and Uncle Ray came for Memorial Day I suggested that we go pick berries. There was not one to be found. Reviewing the spring, my uncle reasoned that a few early warm days had brought out the blooms but no insects to fertilize them. In nature all signals must be "Go" in order to produce. Interrelationships of soil, water, weather, bugs, animals, seeds and nutrients determine the abundance of wild foods even more than that of cultivated foods. Man steps in and fulfills certain needs of a garden, but in nature each plant is on its own.

If you watch the wilderness, each year seems to highlight a different plant. This year we enjoyed abundant wild strawberries. It takes about an hour to pick a quart plus all you can pop into your mouth. I used to tell the kids that anything red was to be put into the bucket, but since the day my husband reached through the leaves and tried to pluck the red band off a strawberry snake, we all carry a stick and look first. Snakes are rare and harmless if they are eating strawberries, but using a stick to push back the leaves quiets apprehension and gives pleasure to picking. I usually carry a walking stick on all my jaunts through the woods; a good stick is invaluable against attacking bulls, spiders and brambles.

An excellent way to de-hull wild strawberries for cooking or raw sauce is to put them into an old nylon stocking, then squeeze as if milking a cow. A nylon stocking with about two cups of berries in the toe and the top tied around the kitchen-sink faucet works fine if there are no runs.

Sugar and cream over cold wild-strawberry pulp make gluttons out of all who fill their sauce dishes with this pleasant dessert. In jam, preserves, pie and shortcake recipes, the substitution of pulp for whole fruit stirs no complaints. The wild fruit seems less watery than cultivated strawberries and the taste is more intense; also, less sugar is needed for most recipes.

We were in the Boston, Virginia, country store near our ranch this past May talking strawberries when a farm wife told us she had baked her husband a "strawberry muffin" that afternoon. She said that when he came in from milking he sat down and ate the whole thing. Her description sounded so good I went back to the cabin and made one with my wild-strawberry mush. Hot, fragrant, at eight-thirty on a frisky spring night, strawberry muffin is superb.

Take one egg, a tablespoon of sugar, one-quarter cup of butter, and beat all together thoroughly. Add one cup of milk, a little salt and one cup of flour into which is sifted two teaspoons of baking powder. When mixed into a stiff batter, add enough flour to make a dough, roll out one-half inch thick and lay the dough into a buttered gingerbread pan. (I used an 8″ x 8″ x 2″ square.) The dough should hang well over each side. Then pour one-and-one-half cups of sweetened wild-strawberry pulp, which has been mixed with two tablespoons of flour, into the center of the big muffin. Pull each hung-over dough side across the top and pinch the corners so that the dough will not leak; the top will not quite be covered. Bake at 400° F. for about thirty minutes and the muffin will become puffy and crisp, with a lush strawberry pudding in the center.

Strawberry ice cream was my grandmother's specialty. She made a huge custard of sixteen eggs and two quarts of milk, into which she stirred a quart of rich cream, poured it into the hand freezer and put me on the turning end. I turned until the dasher began to get stiff and the custard cream was half frozen. Meanwhile, Grandma had mashed and abundantly sweetened two quarts of strawberries. When I ran out of steam, she carefully removed the top from the freezer and with a long-handled spoon beat in the sugary crushed berries. After she replaced the top, I went back to my turning until I could not budge the handle any more. When the ice cream was done, the freezer was packed down in ice and rock salt, and the hardest work of all began—waiting until time to eat.

My most recent triumph with strawberries was wine. A neighbor invited us to share his berries after he had picked all he could use, so, loaded with dishpans, our family moved into his patch. After I had made shortcakes, pies, jams and had canned fourteen quarts in light syrup, I couldn't resist the temptation. I mashed four quarts of strawberries into a crock, covered them with boiling water, permitted them to set for twenty-four hours, then squeezed out the pulp through a muslin sack and discarded it. I added two and a half pounds of sugar to the juice and gently boiled the exquisite liquid for ten minutes. When it cooled, I returned the juice to the crock, filled it with enough boiled water to make one gallon, then put in one cake of yeast that had been dissolved in warm water. This was fermented fourteen days, then skimmed, strained, bottled in sterilized jars, corked lightly for a few weeks, and when the corks stayed down, sealed. A year or so later the result was uncorked and our ruby wine was decanted. Aroma, body, smoothness and taste melded into an illusion of dew-moist strawberries.

Next to strawberries, greens, and liver, I like mushrooms best. But unfortunately, being an unschooled mycologist and a coward to boot, I forage only for puffballs and morels.

When violets and dogwood lend color to the brown earth, morels poke up their wizened heads to look around. Sponge mushrooms, also called miracle plant or morel (*Morchella esculenta*), are one of nature's early spring offerings; so each May I head for the woods and fields to hunt for them.

Morels usually prefer limestone country with a rich humus overlay and grow most eagerly in deciduous forests. As their common name implies, their egg-shaped cap is holed like a sponge. Some are light brown and some are dark, but both cap and stem are hollow and the stem runs through the cap. Their Latin specific name, *esculenta*, means "edible"; that gives me confidence; so I brave raw winds and showers to gather morels, which fortunately keep well under refrigeration.

The foothills of the Blue Ridge, where our small acreage is located, are favored with the miracle plant, as morels are locally called. Unless you are partial to grit, after you cut the mushrooms from their habitat, slice off the bottoms of the stems before tossing the fruits into a basket.

I like morels best with the thick slices simply rinsed, dried and sautéed in butter. If the morels are large, I slice them a half-inch thick and briefly soak them in salted water while butter is melting in a pan, then fry them. Some spring fishermen slice them and toss them into a skillet with frying bacon. Some cooks stuff morels with hamburger and a few onions. One of my friends treats them with diced ham and rice, and they taste like Swedish meatballs, she says.

Alaska grows multitudes of nonpoisonous mushrooms, which Alaskans preserve by drying. We used to briefly brine whole mushrooms, then dry them in the sun or in a low oven. We later strung them on lines and hung them in a dry place for use in ragouts, sauces and stuffings. When mushrooms are dried they do not get stiff; they are rather like a dehydrated ear—tough, pliable and brown.

One neighbor in Virginia cans mushrooms by blanching the washed morels in a boiling water bath, poking them into pint jars to which one-half teaspoon of salt has been added, and filling each jar with boiling water before sealing. She processes the jars for three hours of simmering in her canner.

As May progresses, wild-food foragers forgo their search for greens and concentrate on sprouts.

An internationally syndicated columnist, Philip H. Love, in his column "Love on Life," has proposed poke as our national weed. His SFTPOP, Society for the Propagation of Pokeweed, promotes the eating of poke (*Phytolacca americana*). Correspondents have sent Mr. Love recipes for poke served as a cooked cold salad with hollandaise, poke pickled in vinegar, spice and sugar, poke in a coating of cornmeal and fried in bacon drippings, poke sprouts with scrambled eggs, poke fritters in a batter of garlic and eggs, and poke in cream sauce served on toast.

I enjoy my poke straight, just boiled two or three times, then served with butter, salt and pepper.

Because the mature leaves, roots and inky berries are said to be poisonous, only the young sprouts, those no taller than six inches, should be cooked. They are easy to gather on a bright May day, and cutting them early does not injure the plant. Pokeweed is a coarse herb with alternate, large and elliptically pointed leaves. When the plant matures the tall stems become purplish and bear slender clusters of blackish berries opposite the leaves. The berry stalks often turn bright red. Pokeweed grows in rich open soil from the Great Lakes southward, and the young shoots (the only part of pokeweed that may be safely eaten) poke up from the bases of old woody stalks from April to June.

Pokeweed should be marked during summer, cut the following May, and boiled in at least two waters, because the first water may have a purgative quality.

To my taste, pokeweed combines the flavor and consistency of asparagus with that of spinach.

Milkweed (*Asclepias* family) is another plant sprout that may be eaten in May.

As a sprout, milkweed might be mistaken for the violently emetic dogbane (*Apocynum androsaemifolium*), so it, like pokeweed, should be identified and marked the previous summer so that there is no chance of mix-up. Milkweed leaves are oblong, they grow opposite and they contain a broad midrib. In the summer they bear showy clusters of pinkish flowers that are followed by large green-gray pods bearing silky seeds, which distinctly differentiates milkweed from dogbane. Common milkweed is found in dry, open soil from Canada southward.

Dogbane has a smooth, green, tough pencillate sprout that exudes milk when broken. The stem turns ruddy as the plant matures. Dogbane flowers are loose bells, and the seed pods develop in long narrow pairs. The opposite leaves are elliptically narrow, and dogbane plants fork into a bush rather than grow from one thick stalk as most milkweeds do.

New milkweed shoots are the part to be eaten in May. They

are unbranched and should be cut at ground level while the leaves are unexpanded and the shoots only a few inches high. Milkweed sprouts have a woolly fuzz which may be rubbed off by hand. After they are de-fuzzed and washed, they are dropped into boiling water and cooked like asparagus. I cook milkweed sprouts in two or three waters to remove the bitterness. The shoots turn bright green in the boiling water, and when daubed with butter, salt and pepper, they make a colorful vegetable dish.

I have read that raw milkweed sprouts are poisonous, but cooked they are pleasant-tasting.

My favorite sprout is wild asparagus. Back in Missouri, my grandfather knew exactly where to look for the pale, fat spears. Asparagus grow from rootstocks and may be found in the same place year after year—so, taking his long-bladed fish knife, a bucket, and me, he headed for the bank of a creek, and there we found a multitude of old straw-colored stalks; these were void of fern or berries and looked very much like a miniature forest of leafless trees. At the base of the dried plants, spears and greening asparagus tips protruded through the matted grass and weeds. Reaching his knife under the soil and cutting diagonally, Grandaddy drew out six or seven spears. The old weeds had kept the asparagus pale, and they were so tender we often broke and nibbled one raw, then moved to another and another telltale grouping of old asparagus stalks.

Grandma cooked the washed asparagus about twenty minutes in salted boiling water, then doused them with melted butter, pepper and salt. Sometimes she made a soup. Often she creamed them and served them over toast. For a salad she covered the cooked and cooled spears with a little vinegar, salt, pepper and a sliced hard boiled egg.

I have served wild asparagus, boiled, drained and weeping with butter, by placing them over crisp hot croutons and sprinkling them with grated Parmesan cheese.

We have seven clumps of wild asparagus on our ranch in

Virginia. Some give one fat spear, some give a handful of finger-sized tips, some are pencil-thin. Our garden asparagus sprout a little earlier than the wild ones (I suspect this is because I clear brush from the beds) but when both ripen at the same time, I mix them and cannot tell the difference.

Bracken, or fiddlehead fern (*Pteridium aquilinum*), is another sprout-type wild food. Bracken is a coarse fern with a single thick base stalking into three distinct curled fronds several inches from the ground, and it grows in low, moist land from Canada southward into Virginia. To cut them, the coiled fiddleheads are snapped off. Their coat of fuzz is easily rubbed off by pulling each head through your hand. Bracken are usually cooked in boiling water for about a half-hour, seasoned with pepper and salt and dressed with melted butter, oil and vinegar, or sour cream. These fern heads may be nibbled raw—some people enjoy their slickity quality—but I prefer fiddlehead fern sprouts cooked like asparagus or fresh green beans. Mature fronds of bracken are reputed to be toxic to grazing animals, but as long as the ferns are coiled and tender, they are edible by man.

Flowers of May are, I believe, the most glorious creations of God. Though I get nostalgic over chrysanthemums in the fall, and lighthearted with the first daffodil, I experience a sustained pleasure each May when the earth blooms.

Part of the joy is because you can savor and save May bouquets. Daisy, rose, honeysuckle, apple and clover, all may be captured in blossom wines, sachets and confections.

Daisy wine is my very favorite because I love to make it. There is a hint of eternal youth in skipping through meadows or along the edge of the golf course plucking daisies. One Indian tribe holds the daisy as a symbol of love and happiness, and I like the idea of putting that into bottles. I have read that some Indians sprinkle the marriage bed with daisy petals and that their maidens wear daisies in their hair as a betrothal pledge.

Daisy wine is a topaz pledge with a teasing taste.

Cover four quarts of field-daisy blossoms (*Chrysanthemum leucanthemum*) with a gallon of boiling water and let stand for twenty-four hours. Squeeze out the daisies and gently boil the liquid with two lemons and two oranges, all thinly sliced, and three pounds of brown sugar for twenty minutes. Cool and add one-half box of raisins, a knuckle of ginger root or a teaspoon of ginger powder which has been tied in a tiny sack, and one package of softened yeast. Allow to ferment for about fourteen days in a covered crock, strain, bottle in sterilized jars, and cap lightly. About two months later, seal and store until your friends' daughters are married, then toast their happiness.

What May evening, the air heavy with honeysuckle, can fail to enchant? Honeysuckle wine charms the palate as completely as the limpid fragrance of the bloom entrances the senses. Amber and heavy, honeysuckle wine exudes emotion. I have to be careful whom I serve this wine to.

Pick one gallon of honeysuckle flowers, or pick until your fingers become so silken with pollen you cannot grasp any more flowers, then cover the blossoms with one gallon of boiling water. Simmer for twenty minutes, cool, strain, discard the blossoms and add enough boiling water to the remaining liquid to make one gallon. Stir in two-and-a-half pounds of sugar, two cups of white raisins, two sliced lemons and one package of yeast which has been dissolved in one cup of water. Toss in two bruised ginger roots, each about an inch long, cover and let ferment for approximately two weeks. (I stir this daily because it makes the basement smell good.) I strain the honeysuckle wine into sterilized bottles and cork it lightly. When the bubbles no longer run up the side of the bottle when I touch it lightly (in about two months), I seal each bottle with paraffin.

Honeysuckle is a gay wine and should be opened for a merry toast with neighbors.

Rose petals create a delicate spring wine and are numerous around old homesteads. Pour one gallon of boiling water over three or four quarts of roses (no green or poison-sprayed roses or bugs), add the cut-up rind of two oranges and three pounds of sugar. Boil for twenty minutes, cool, strain, and add a package of yeast which has been dissolved in warm water, the juice from the oranges, and four or five peppercorns. Let ferment in a covered crock for about fourteen days, strain, discard petals and bottle in sterilized jars, cork lightly for three months or until the wine has finished working, then seal each bottle with paraffin.

Rose wine is a pleasure to serve the following spring when roses bloom again. I have served pink buttonhole-rose wine with lunch and decorated the room with the same climbers.

My grandmother had great faith in roses. She often said a good mother will rise like the scent of roses straight to heaven. In May the brilliance of her yard drew visitors from miles away. Maybe they believed that they might be borne to heaven on the fragrance of her roses.

Grandma believed that tea made from petals of red roses would expel "womanly melancholy and cure madness." She may have said that facetiously, but I can remember her picking large red roses for her female visitors. First she "shook out the tears," if dew or rain was on them, and then she put them into a teapot and poured boiling water on them. The visitors would sit and sip the fragrant tea, as they talked endlessly. They always seemed to be more relaxed as they left our house, saying gentle words about the miracles of roses.

Grandma made tea-rose-petal preserves that looked as if the sun's rays were in each jar.

She made rose pancakes by dipping a pinch of large petals into heavy sweet wine, then into a flour-egg-and-milk batter. She fried the battered petals in butter and served them with powdered sugar.

Grandma pickled small rosebuds by loosely packing them into sterilized half-pint jars and quickly pouring over them a boiling sweet-pickle juice. She sealed the jars and stored them for winter salads or for relishes with sandwiches.

Each May Grandma would pluck the petals of fresh red roses and dry them on window screens placed between two chairs in the sun. In three or four days, when they were thoroughly dry, she would pack them into jars and cover them tightly to retain their fragrance. She would treat lavender, lemon verbena, rose geraniums and rosemary in the same manner and then make sweet bags. She put a handful of dried flowers into the center of a piece of silk, then gathered up the edges and stitched on a bit of ribbon to make sachets. Sometimes Grandma made her sachets more exotic by adding such exciting spices as whole cloves, cinnamon, allspice, ginger and bergamot leaves. She said spices discouraged paper weevils.

Grandma said a miniature pillow filled with dried flowers, peppermint, rosemary and sweet woodruff would keep away moths. She did not believe in camphor.

To get rid of stuffy smells in her parlor, Grandma kept a rose jar. (I don't think the windows opened.) She took a quart of dried rose petals, pink, yellow and red, one pint of dried geranium leaves, one pint of dried lavender flowers, one pint of dried rosemary, and she mixed them all with a little plain salt, ground cinnamon, allspice, anise seed, nutmeg, cloves, ginger and two tablespoons of powdered orris root. She capped the big jar tightly for two months, and then, before company came, she took off the lid. The spicy scent transformed our front room into a fragrant, enchanting place. I felt like a princess and wanted to wear my best dress to saunter through the portieres. Sweet, spicy odors tell me wonderful things.

Blossoms and bees go together. The blooms of May are best for making honey, according to a doctor I once worked for.

Dr. Sorenson dispensed his own medicine, and though he used modern drugs, he also used honey to a considerable extent.

A teaspoonful of honey at bedtime was prescribed as a sedative for children. He winked at the words but vowed that a tuck-in and honey worked psychological wonders.

MAY

I prepared many bottles of glycerine and honey with a sprinkle of rose extract for chapped hands, and the doctor gave it to harassed housewives as he listened to their woes.

He considered sassafras bark infused and mixed with honey to be a pickup for "burned-out blood."

For rheumatic complaints he prescribed a pinch of caraway seeds sprinkled into a cup of boiling water in which a tablespoon each of honey and lemon juice had been dissolved.

For coughs he recommended an extract of pine and honey. He also had me boil small pieces of oat straw and then add honey to create a soothing cold remedy.

Strawberry leaves, boiled and strained, the liquid then taken with honey as a mild tea, were prescribed for minor liver complaints.

Sweet basil tea with honey clears throat and sinus congestion, he said.

A pinch of rosemary floated on a teaspoonful of honey and taken at lunch time, he said, was beneficial for nervous headaches.

He used ashes from burned linden wood, one teaspoonful with one teaspoonful of honey in a cup of warm milk, for people with digestive disorders.

To help soothe motherly nerves, he prescribed bergamot tea with honey at four o'clock each afternoon, "with the feet up."

Dr. Sorenson had started practicing medicine long before artificial chemical preparations had begun to replace natural remedies. He did not hesitate to prescribe modern drugs, but at the same time he had faith in certain old medicines and in the honey from "happy bees."

Honey wine or mead was a traditional drink of Vikings, warlocks and honeymooners, but it was a quiet drink of gentle folk in history, too.

My grandfather made a golden mead with dark honey, which he called "Promise." He used old honey, and if it had crystallized, he would place the opened jars in a dishpan of warm water and gradually heat them. When they were warmed through he would slip racks under the jars and put the whole thing on the cookstove to simmer until the honey was liquid.

For Promise, three or four pounds of strained honey were combined with a gallon of water and slowly boiled in an enamel kettle for three minutes, then skimmed and cooled. A box of muscat raisins, an orange and a lemon, sliced, and the slightly beaten whites of two eggs were stirred into the honey-water mixture, and a package of fresh yeast dissolved in a cup of warm water was added. The mead crock was covered and allowed to ferment behind the stove with a daily stirring for about three weeks. The mead was strained, bottled in sterilized containers, corked lightly, and when all fermentation stopped, sealed tight. Though somewhat flatter than wine, this mead was satisfying with a meal.

Mead may be made with plain honey and water, but because honey contains little acid and tannin, both citric acid and tea should be added if no fruit is used. The best fermentation temperature for mead is between 60° and 70° F. If it becomes warmer than that it is likely to stop fermenting prematurely or "stick."

Mead not only "sticks" if it becomes too warm; it will also stop working if it becomes too cold or if the mixture does not contain sufficient tannin or acid. Mead which has not completed fermentation has a tendency to blow up in bottles. My grandmother's best bleeding-heart plant was cut down one year by Grandaddy's exploding Promise.

Mead may be made with flowers such as rose petals, dandelions, elder, clover or apple blossoms, or with most fruits.

I made mead recently when our daughter returned from Hawaii bearing two succulent pineapples. I mixed three-and-a-half pounds of light honey with a gallon of hot water and simmered it for three minutes.

After we had eaten those gorgeous fruits I added the

chopped peelings of the two pineapples and one cup of strong, freshly made tea. When the mixture cooled, I added a package of yeast and the slightly beaten whites of two eggs. I covered the crock and put it into a warm place for about two weeks. When the action seemed subdued, I strained the mead, bottled it in sterilized bottles and corked it lightly. In two or three months, when all fermentation has stopped, I will seal it and let it mellow another two or three months to develop a bouquet of the Islands.

This mead will be less full-flavored than my grandfather's, but it will hold the fierce beauty of an Hawaiian sunset. I know because I have already tasted it.

Some people deposit a honeybee in each bottle of mead— this says "Luck to the recipient." I got the bee once but I couldn't bring myself to swallow it. The insect had obviously had a happy death. One wing was tethered under its chin and it seemed to wave at me as I sipped mead from my glass.

May brings blossoms and sprouts to the wildland; in the garden, new seed life emerges; to man May brings warmth, and for those who will let themselves feel, the earth blooms.

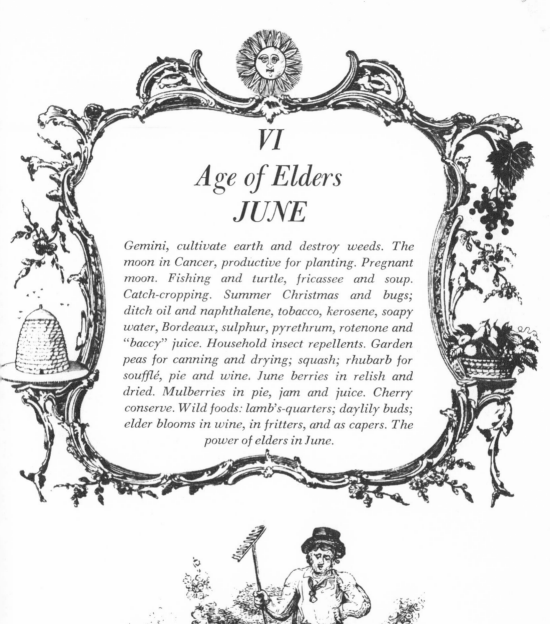

VI
Age of Elders
JUNE

Gemini, cultivate earth and destroy weeds. The moon in Cancer, productive for planting. Pregnant moon. Fishing and turtle, fricassee and soup. Catch-cropping. Summer Christmas and bugs; ditch oil and naphthalene, tobacco, kerosene, soapy water, Bordeaux, sulphur, pyrethrum, rotenone and "baccy" juice. Household insect repellents. Garden peas for canning and drying; squash; rhubarb for soufflé, pie and wine. June berries in relish and dried. Mulberries in pie, jam and juice. Cherry conserve. Wild foods: lamb's-quarters; daylily buds; elder blooms in wine, in fritters, and as capers. The power of elders in June.

GEMINI AND HIS BARREN ARMS rule the soil until June 21. Pull weeds, destroy noxious growth, turn sod, especially during the fourth or last quarter of the moon, my grandfather would say. When the fourth quarter of the moon is combined with the airy, barren, dry and masculine zodiac sign of Gemini, plants may be most effectively destroyed, moon-sign followers believe. I met a farmer who cut locust, maple and oak from his woodlot under that sign and declared that the stumps would not sprout. Other farmers put down fence posts during the last quarter of the moon under Gemini, saying that the posts would not rot. My grandfather cultivated his garden early each June, and I, too, find that a young garden needs weeding and cultivation at that time.

If green beans, squash or cabbage are leggy, the earth should be pulled up around their stalks in June before they bloom or head. Onions, beets and turnips should be hilled up under the sign of Gemini (May 21 to June 21) too. Potatoes should be hilled up before they bloom.

To hill up, you hoe the dirt up around the base of the plant in order to cover the root as well as to support the plant. If potatoes grow too close to the surface they may sunburn; that means they turn green on the surface side—and sunburned potatoes, like sunburned people, are bitter. Although potatoes grow best buried in loose soil, do not work the earth around potato plants while they are blooming. I did that once; the result was lovely plants but no potatoes.

Cancer (June 21 to July 22) is believed by zodiac gardeners to be the most productive time for planting. Leftover seeds and seedlings may be popped into the ground under Cancer with a good chance of maturing. I have talked with moon-sign believers who customarily wait for the appropriate phase of the moon under Cancer to finish planting their main garden.

They watch for a pregnant moon, too, as a bonus. If the first quarter of the moon coincided with the first days under the sign of Cancer, my grandfather called it a pregnant moon. I was always confused about this because when he announced its pregnancy the moon was the merest sliver.

A pregnant moon in June was considered an excellent garden sign. When this phenomenon was scheduled to occur, Grandaddy saved a space to plant a special garden, a small planting of nearly every aboveground crop. He said the plants would bear in nine weeks, according to the natural cycle. He also predicted that rains would be adequate to support the late planting, and that the following winter would be severe.

I have watched for a pregnant moon, but in my Mixmaster suburban life I have not been able to make empirical observations, formulate a working hypothesis, collect, record and classify data and apply generalizations. Logical reasoning suggests skepticism, but the basic principles of research have not been applied so I cannot evaluate the pregnant-moon theory.

Uncle Steve always tried to set eggs so that they would hatch under the fruitful sign of Cancer because he said the pullets would mature more rapidly and be better layers. "Even the roosters are fat and juicy," he would say, winking, as he described the merits of late June hatchings.

Grandaddy sometimes grafted trees during Cancer's sign. He put together one tree that bore three kinds of plums, and the poor thing didn't know whether it was a damson, a yellow or a big purple.

My grandfather would never paint during the watery sign of Cancer. "Won't dry," he would tell Grandma; then he would take his gear and go fishing. Red horse, log perch, and sunfish—in fact, most fish—bite better during the wet signs, Grandaddy said.

JUNE

Our family has been always ready to wet a line, wet sign or no. One June, my husband, the kids (then toddlers) and I went fishing in the Hazel River near our Culpeper County cabin. Suddenly, in the overflow pool, our son, Martin, spied a snapping turtle. Big as a basketball, he said, and insisted that we come look.

Sure enough! The finest snapper we had seen dozed in the Virginia sun.

Primitive urges sprang into gear.

We stationed our two girls at the overflow with sticks and the boy at the pond intake with a club. My husband said that my job was to shove a stick into the snapper's jaws when he grabbed it by the tail.

With one sweep my trusting husband yanked the monster aloft. The turtle was indignant. Its cumbersome body swung in wide arcs as it tried to bite. Its jaws snapped like a rat trap, but it whirled so fast I could not get my stick into its mouth. The children were frightened and they fled as Lewis kept swinging the turtle in circles shouting, "Shove it in!"

At last he dropped the flailing beast into a tiny rain pool on the top of the rock outcropping, and when it tried to crawl out, Lewis shoved the stick into the turtle's mouth. Hanging by its jaws, the snapper allowed itself to be placed into our cooler chest. We tied the lid down and carried the chest to the cabin, where we released the turtle into the wash-tub.

Our prize quiescent after a skirmish or two over the sides, we all buzzed about building a fire, sharpening knives and filling the big canner kettle with water. When the water in the canner came to a full rolling boil, we gave the snapping turtle his stick, stretched his neck over a stump, and *whomp!*

Quickly grabbing the tail, Lewis popped the decapitated turtle into the boiling water, and one minute later took it out and flopped it onto the paper-covered outdoors table.

He severed the skin close to the back shell and lifted the back shell off. He turned the turtle over and removed the lower plate in the same manner. After immersion in boiling water, both shells are easily removed.

With a sharp, pointed knife my husband next cut the soft belly flesh midline, removed the entrail much as he would clean a fish, then, making four slits from the incision down the inside of each leg, he cut away the skin. He peeled the coarse outer skin from the body and cut it from the meat along with the neck, tail and feet. The turtle skin peeled almost as easily as peeling a banana to expose pale pink muscles of meat. There was very little blood and, after we rolled up the newspapers, no odor or disagreeable sight. Lewis divided the carcass into four pieces, approximately two pounds each, and refrigerated the meat overnight.

I fricasseed the first quarter of turtle by cubing the meat, dousing it with flour, then browning it and covering it with cold water. I added salt, pepper, a little minced onion and catsup, then simmered it for one-and-a-half hours. Actually the time was too long, because the meat fell apart. The major problem in cooking wild game is determining age. Our snapper, though a big, rough-looking fellow, was apparently quite young.

For the gravy I blended a tablespoon of browned flour into a paste with a tablespoon of butter, then mixed it with the liquid in the pan, added a glass of sherry, and very gradually stirred in the yolk of one egg. This was brought to a boil and a can of undiluted cream of mushroom soup was tossed in. The whole thing was simmered for three minutes and then turned into a heated deep dish into which the turtle meat had been spooned. The rich gravy seeped through and moistened the meat. Served with rice, that was a good meal.

The second quarter of our turtle I pan-fried as I would fry chicken, for about thirty minutes on each side, and I had to slam on the skillet cover to keep it from jumping out of the pan. Like frogs' legs, turtle meat "lives till the sun goes down."

Uncle Steve used to say snapper contained seven kinds of

meat. He was partial to white meat. He said the dark leg muscles tasted like clam and the brisket like lamb. My taste buds must not be so discerning. Robust in flavor, turtle meat is mildly reminiscent of ocean shores, with a clean, meat taste.

One bowl of turtle soup makes a hearty meal. I made one type of turtle soup with tomatoes and vegetables, another with milk, butter and a little cayenne.

Grandma canned turtle meat just once. During the drought years, when the creeks were drying up, Grandaddy transported dozens of small snappers to the river. The big turtles we ate, and Grandma canned some just as she canned chicken. The following winter the canned turtle made into tasty stew and goulash. For goulash she boiled cabbage, potatoes, onions and a little smoked bacon with the meat, and she added about a teaspoon of paprika to each quart.

Home gardens begin to pay off in June. Radishes, lettuce, green onions, peas, summer squash, greens and beans seem to explode into maturity overnight. I have noticed that youngsters do that, too, with one major difference: they are children one day and young adults the next, and vice versa. Adolescents do not explode into maturity and stay mature like proper vegetables.

To run an efficient garden (which I have yet to do), certain plantings are staggered; that is, specific vegetables are replanted every few weeks to insure continued fresh produce; also, efficient gardeners plant catch-crops. Catch-cropping means that quick-growing crops are sown and harvested before the time when late crops must be planted. For example, lettuce may be harvested and late cabbage planted in the same ground, or turnips may be planted after the main crop of potatoes has been dug.

These practices save space and face. I planted carrots one time, had no patience weeding the dumb things, yanked them all out, and catch-cropped kohlrabi. When we decided we didn't like kohlrabi, I pulled them up and planted lettuce, which the birds ate. Who was it said, "If you can't amuse 'em, confuse 'em"? A garden is a wonderful outlet for confusion.

Sweet potatoes and peanuts are excellent catch-croppers. Any four-legged deer in the area will eat the sweet-potato vines, and you can enjoy the wildlife. Most kids love to raise peanuts even if they get only one handful to roast.

When we celebrated "Summer Christmas," June 26, which was also the name day of St. John the Baptist, my grandfather called upon the saint to assist him in his fight against garden insects, diseases and weeds. Grandaddy maintained that the bounty of a natural year was God's gift to man, and he intended to help the good Lord in every way he could.

A balanced hoe and a strong back, Uncle Steve said, would take care of weeds, but he waged his own private war on bugs. He mustered his own militia (me) and stockpiled his weapons with great care.

On a still, dry morning, I helped to carry buckets of old engine oil, soapsuds and salt water, "baccy juice," kerosene and naphthalene flakes, while he carried the poisons, duster, spray and hand plow to the garden.

En route Grandaddy would describe the particular types of bugs or diseases he was attacking. I learned about chewing insects, such as the Mexican bean beetle; suckers, such as aphis or plant lice; fungus, such as blight; and boring insects, which injure trees and roots.

My grandfather sprayed or dusted the cultivated garden about three times during a summer, but I seemed to be always picking beetles. Of course I got paid. Ten potato bugs were worth a cent; bean beetles were six for a penny; five stinkbugs removed from squash went for a cent.

Caterpillars, cutworms and slugs were good for fishing. For them, I carried a coffee can with a screen top. I earned a penny for every two pieces of fish bait.

Before starting to dust or spray, we picked a mess of greens, peas, onions, or any other produce that was ripe.

My grandfather then plowed a sharp furrow around the

garden and drizzled old engine oil and naphthalene (beta naphthol) all along the ditch. This, he said, would discourage invading plant lice, thrips, army worms, snakes, snails, moles and mice. Sometimes he laid old tobacco stalks in the trench. He said aphis hate tobacco. When aphis come in contact with nicotine dust or tobacco, they turn somersaults and leave.

In addition, Grandaddy used a kerosene emulsion on the underside of young bean plants to do away with the bean aphis. He had faith in coal oil, as he called his kerosene spray. A half-pound of hard kitchen soap was shredded into a gallon of boiling water, dissolved, and added to two gallons of kerosene. He diluted this ten to one with water and sprayed it on all plants that showed leaf curl but were not yet in the edible stage. He was careful not to spill his kerosene emulsion on cabbages or greens.

Grandaddy believed soapy laundry water mixed with a mild salt solution, one-quarter cup of salt to two quarts of soapy water, doused regularly over cabbages and kale would turn off sucking insects and eliminate caterpillars and moths. Many Monday evenings we showered the cabbages with buckets of the "clean" soapy water Grandma saved from the wash. The "dirty" wash water was used to scrub the back porch. When soapy water was not available, we dusted the cabbages with plain wheat flour. Grandaddy said flour discouraged the little yellow or white butterflies.

Root maggots in onions, cabbage and turnip-type plants and bean-leaf beetles were controlled by laying the tobacco leaves along each row. Sometimes Grandaddy mixed calomel (mercurous chloride) with lime and spread it at the base of root crop plants to ward off grubs.

Fungus was treated once a season with a Bordeaux mixture. For Bordeaux, my grandfather mixed one pound of copper sulphate with a gallon of water in one enamel pan and one pound of hydrated lime with a gallon of water in another. For a general garden fungicide he mixed one part of the lime solution to one part of the copper sulfate solution to twelve-

and-a-half parts of water, and he sprayed at once.

If white mildew coatings appeared on the leaves, they were dusted with sulphur.

Next to crows, chewing insects were always Grandaddy's biggest problem. The crows knew he was softhearted and they took advantage of him, but the dumb bugs stupidly ate their way into bug heaven. To help control chewing insects my grandfather posted a birdhouse for purple martins near his garden. He also dusted the plants with pyrethrum powder and sulphur. He used one part pyrethrum powder (Dalmatian or Persian insect powder made from the dried flower of a variety of painted daisy, *Chrysanthemum cinearaefolium*) to nine parts sulphur. This mixture was suitable for dusting on edible vegetables, he said. He also dusted the chicken-roosting areas with pyrethrum and sulphur to cut down on the housefly population.

Grandaddy tried planting painted daisies around the garden one year; the blooms looked nice, but the bugs didn't leave.

Rotenone, made from the crushed root of the pea-vine derris, was my grandfather's second weapon against chewing insects. For general use he mixed rotenone with sulphur one to nine, and he sometimes combined rotenone with pyrethrum powder for a particularly heavy infestation of beetles or worms. A stomach and contact poison, rotenone is said to be nonpoisonous to man, but an insect killer.

Grandaddy was ahead of his time regarding the fear of water pollution. When he found that rotenone killed fish, that was the end of that poison for him. He avoided the lead-arsenate poisons, then popular as potato-plant sprays, because he believed that rains would carry arsenic to the rivers and in time fresh water would be contaminated.

Uncle Steve's most famous pest repellent, however, was his "baccy juice." He used it on nonedible parts of plants for suckers, chewers and ordinary bugs just passing through the garden. His spot for making "baccy juice" was off the far end of the back porch under the wisteria arbor. Grandma said the juice smelled like a copper spittoon and would not allow the mess near her kitchen. To make the repellent Grandaddy put about three-quarters of a bushel of imperfect tobacco leaves saved from last year's crop into a washtub and covered them with boiling water. He mashed the ugly brown slop for about an hour with a wooden paddle, then let it cool.

While my grandfather advocated some poisons for specific and serious plant infestations, and often cited the potato blight and its control by fungicides, he was opposed to habitual spraying of gardens.

My grandfather believed that plant health was directly related to sunshine. He did not crowd, nor did he hesitate to thin. I am often reluctant to thin plants, and my husband has to sneak into the garden and thin when I am not looking. To me each plant is like my own offspring and I cannot bear ripping them out, even though I know that crowding encourages weakness, bugs and disease.

In the house, Grandma put rosemary among her woolens as a moth preventative. She rubbed fennel as a flea powder behind the cat's ears, and sprinkled crushed tobacco leaves mixed with fennel and rosemary powder as a flea and moth repellent in woolen rugs. Red pepper, fennel and borax were spread on ant runways, and spearmint herbs were hung in the pantry and cellars because she believed mints discouraged rats and flies. Grandaddy gathered the wild spearmint from nearby stream banks, where he also gathered green elder leaves which he crushed and rubbed on his arms and neck as an insect repellent.

As June progresses, a vegetable garden provides more and more varieties of food. In addition to harvests of sweet greens such as beet tops, chard, kale, spinach and turnip tassels, salad makings are abundant. Green beans sometimes throw an early crop, and summer squash often lurk golden under their leaves. It is always an adventure to walk through the garden to see what's new. True, there are disappointments, but they are offset by surprises. Rarely does a garden "freak out."

Green peas are usually rated as the ultimate crop during June. Weekend gardeners seldom experience the treat of fresh garden peas because the country varmints are on the spot to harvest seven days a week, and Friday-night-to-Sunday-afternooners haven't got a chance. Also, peas demand lots of space and postage-stamp gardeners have little room for the land-hungry legumes.

Peas must be picked when the pods are full but not leathery, in the morning after the sun has dried the soil, then shelled immediately and dumped into boiling water. Fresh peas embody all the sweetness of the earth when they are cooked within thirty minutes after they are picked, my grandmother said.

Late pea plants should be mulched and treated with nitrogen-rich fertilizer. My grandfather used chicken droppings to fertilize his garden and he dressed the peas especially heavily with it. If the weather is not too hot, a late pea crop may fool the local wildlife, we have found. They have their rabbit mouths all set for beans, so it is possible to sneak a pea for yourself.

Surplus peas are best frozen, but Grandma used to can them in pints by blanching the shelled fresh peas in boiling water for three to five minutes, then pouring them into hot, sterilized jars. She added a half teaspoon of salt, covered them with boiling water and sealed the jars. She processed pints of peas in a boiling-water bath for three hours. Peas are low-acid, she said, and spoil readily, so she never canned them in quarts because she could not get the inside temperature high enough to kill bacteria.

I used to shell peas with a pea podder, which resembled a miniature clothes wringer. Sitting on the floor with my back to a corner, I fed the pods between the rollers. Peas popped everywhere, and I would duck when they shot back at me.

Grandma also dried peas. She left the last picking on the

vines until the plants were yellow and limp. Dried pea plants should be pulled before a thundershower if they are ready, because rain pops pods open. Ordinarily Grandma pulled the vines on a dry day, then hulled the peas and laid the somewhat dried legumes on a screen in the sun. Each evening she took the screens inside, not so much to evade moisture as to outsmart thieves. One morning when she had forgotten to take in the screens, we awoke to find every bluejay in northwest Missouri holding a pea-pecking convention on the drying frames. Sun-dried peas should be heated in a low oven, 180° F., for thirty minutes to destroy moth and weevil growth.

Another jolly June vegetable is squash. Summer squash, sliced, dipped in flour, and fried like eggplant, is my family's favorite warm-weather supper when served with a slice of ham or a hot dog. I cook a heaping platter of the golden discs and they disappear. I have canned summer squash, but although they add color to storage shelves, they are not much on taste. Fresh squash will keep well in a cool place for three or four weeks.

Some people snicker at the name of a rather commonplace June plant: rhubarb. But rhubarb is simple to grow, simple to pull, simple to cook, and makes simply wonderful pies, sauces and wines.

Rhubarb is said to have come from Asia. Monks introduced it into Europe and prescribed it for the treatment of dysentery. The leaves of rhubarb (*Rheum officinale, Polygonaceae*) contain oxalic acid and should not be eaten. The stalks are delicious as a cooked fruit, in pie, sauce, English tarts and jam.

Rhubarb grows readily in rich garden soil, and five or six plants will supply a family with this early fruit. The plants are perennial and like asparagus they grow best from roots rather than from seed. Rhubarb takes little care. I loosen the soil around the plants from time to time, pull the weeds and fertilize twice a year.

My grandmother made a rhubarb soufflé that was supreme.

Soak half a cup of crumbled bread in a cup of milk while you beat six egg yolks until they are light. Stir in two tablespoons of sugar, then mix the eggs into the sloppy bread. Add a cup of stewed and sweetened rhubarb and fold in the beaten egg whites. Bake in a greased and covered pudding dish for one-half hour, then uncover and brown. Serve warm with sweetened whipped cream.

If I am in a hurry to get out of the cabin in the country and need a quick dessert, I cut up five stalks of rhubarb, mix a cup and a quarter of sugar with a quarter-cup of flour and a pinch of salt, then toss the dry ingredients into the cut-up rhubarb. Mix until lumpy, then pop the whole gooey mess into a pie shell, dot with butter, cover with pastry, seal, poke holes in the crust and bake for an hour at 375° F.

In my house such a pie takes twenty minutes to put together and the pan is licked clean in five minutes after a dinner of beef and potatoes.

Rhubarb may be canned easily. Allow three-fourths pound of sugar to one pound of fruit cut into one-inch pieces, boil and stir continuously for fifteen minutes; fill hot, sterilized pint jars, seal and process thirty minutes in a boiling-water bath.

I have made a plain rhubarb wine by putting a gallon of slushy rhubarb sauce into a crock with two quarts of warm water, four pounds of sugar and a package of dissolved yeast. This mixture is fermented for ten days, a box of raisins is added, and it is all fermented two weeks more. Then strain through a cloth, bottle in sterilized jars, cork lightly, and when fermentation stops, seal. I have made that rhubarb wine only once. A bit tart, it makes an excellent dry, pink wine.

Grandaddy added a quart of dried black elderberries to his rhubarb wine recipe which gave it a mysterious darkness. I do not remember the taste.

Moon-sign followers say that it is best to can or preserve food under the dry and barren zodiac signs, optimumly during the fourth quarter of the moon. If the moon's daily sign is controlled by a dry constellation, that is also considered acceptable for canning. Wine, however, should be made under fruitful signs, and during the waxing, first or second quarter of the moon, my grandfather advised.

June is not complete without hunting for a Juneberry bush. Few wild fruits are as tasty and as easy to gather as Juneberries, or as unfamiliar to contemporary man. Juneberries (*Amelanchier*), also called shadberries, serviceberries or Indian pears, grow in open woods from British Columbia to Newfoundland and south to Mexico. Some are twenty-foot trees with smooth gray bark; some are low shrubs. Their leaves are oblong, somewhat round, and coarsely toothed like apple leaves. Their starlike flowers have five white pointed petals, and the smooth berries are purplish-black or reddish, with well-defined blossom remnants at the distal ends. Some Juneberries droop on thin stems in clusters of five and some are single fruits. Some are thumbnail-sized and others are the size of peas. All are edible.

The easiest time to identify Juneberries is in the early spring. At the same time that the silver maples are putting out their squiggly red flowers, Juneberries bloom. It is best to mark Juneberry bushes when they are in bloom and then come back in June or July to steal their fruit.

My grandmother used Juneberries to make a cranberry-type relish which she called spiced berries. We ate it with roast duck or game. To make a few pints of this sprightly relish, wash two quarts of Juneberries and put them into a pan with a cup of cold water. Tie in a small cheesecloth bag a dozen cloves, a dozen allspice, four sticks of cinnamon (broken) and several blades of mace. Put this bag into the Juneberries and water and stew together until the fruit breaks into bits. Remove the spice bag and rub the berries through a colander, return the pulp to a heavy pot, and add about two-and-three-quarters cups of brown sugar. Boil slowly, stirring regularly until thick, then pour at once into sterilized pint jars and seal.

Juneberries are excellent eaten as a sauce or made into pies. When used in muffins, Juneberries should be stewed gently first, then drained and carefully added to the batter.

Juneberries are simple to dry. The berries are washed, rinsed briefly in a mild brine (a quarter-cup of salt to two quarts of water), and dried for one day on a screen in the sun. (My grandmother's drying screens were painted with enamel to prevent fruit acids from touching metal.) The second day, or when the berries started to lose their plumpness, the berries were mashed for a short time in a colander and the excess juice removed.

At this point Grandma took the pulp by tablespoonfuls, plopped it into small cakes on a smooth board, and set the board in the sun. If flies were out, she laid a veil of cheese-cloth over the fruit. Sometimes she turned the blobs with a spatula. When the cakes felt spongy dry, but firm, like raisins, she put them into sterilized pint jars, separating each cake with a circle of wax paper, and she sealed the jars.

Setting the pemmican-filled jars on a rack in a basting pan in a low oven, 150° F., she heated them very slowly, gradually elevating the heat and holding them at 200° F. for three hours. She then let the jars cool in the oven. If the jars were heated or cooled any faster, they might explode, she explained.

Sometimes Grandma mixed strawberries, raspberries or dewberries with her Juneberry pemmican. When serving them as holiday treats, she rolled the dried cakes in powdered sugar.

Juneberries may be canned as a sauce, sweetened slightly, and processed like any acid fruit.

Mulberries (*Morus rubra* or *M. alba*) are a misunderstood fruit. Although black and red mulberry trees are native to this continent and grow in mixed woods from New England southward, the imported white mulberry seems to be the best known, and also the least tasty. Maybe that accounts for the lack of mulberry popularity. I have seen hundreds of mulberry trees literally dripping fruit allowed to go to waste, and sometimes even cursed by homeowners because of their underfoot mess.

To most tastes, mulberries do not rank with strawberries, but properly prepared they make tasty pies, jams and summer drinks. Generally speaking, mulberries need a touch of lemon juice to add zest to their flavor. My grandmother made a wonderful rhubarb-and-mulberry pie. She mixed cut-up rhubarb with stemmed mulberries, one-and-a-half cups each, with three tablespoons of flour, one cupful of sugar and a pinch of salt; she then poured the mixture into a pie pan lined with pie dough and dotted it with butter. She added a top crust, cut steam openings and baked the pie at 425° F. for thirty to forty-five minutes. The rhubarb makes the pie tart and the mulberries add color and depth.

Mulberries are easily gathered by shaking a tree limb over an old shower curtain. However, they are fragile and do not keep long. Also, a stem in the center of each berry discourages many of today's instant cooks.

I sometimes chill a bowlful and serve them sprinkled with lemon juice for finger food with lunch. Most big people and all little people love them.

Mulberries make a fine jam when they are mashed through a colander and blended with lemon and commercial pectin or green apples as a thickening agent.

Native peoples throughout the world dry them on racks in the sun, or make a paste of the mulberries and dry them in cakes. Care must be taken that flies do not blow them, and if in doubt, the mulberries should be put into a low oven for a few minutes, then returned to the sun and dried under cheesecloth.

A Czech friend told me that her family makes a refreshing drink from mulberry juice and ginger ale. She squeezes the berries through a cheesecloth, then combines one quart of the strained raw mulberry juice with three-fourths cup of sugar and one quart of ginger ale.

In my opinion the American mulberry tree should not be given second-class status merely because it is messy and listless in taste. With a little acid and ingenuity, mulberry flavor can be enhanced and promoted as a nutritious foodstuff for many Americans.

Most wild cherries do not ripen until midsummer, but some escaped cultivated cherries ripen in the June woods. As with Juneberries, it is advisable to locate and mark cherry trees when they bloom in April.

A pleasantly sour wild red cherry that my grandfather called bird-cherry (*Prunus pensylvanica*) ripened in Missouri in June. I remember helping to pit them and Grandaddy saying that cherry pits contained a mild poison. There is a temptation to ferment cherries whole for wine but unless you wish to slowly poison your drinking cohorts, cherries should be pitted before use, he said. I have seen hogs devour cherries by the bucketful and not show discomfort, but then I can't tell a discomforted hog grunt from a comfortable grunt. Bird-cherries make fine jelly and the thin pulp quenches thirst when the cherries are eaten raw.

My grandmother had a "company shelf" in the cellar which was arrayed with festive marmalades, party pickles and fancy canned goods. I remember studying the shelf longingly, and Grandma's cherry conserve was the gayest jar to catch my yearning eye.

For conserve, wash, pick over and pit one quart of cherries, add one quart of currants (or a box of plumped raisins), one pint of raspberries and one thinly sliced orange. Weigh the fruit and add an equal amount of sugar. Let it come to a boil slowly in a heavy pot, then boil rapidly until thick. Add one-half pound of English walnuts and pour into hot, sterilized jelly glasses; seal with paraffin.

Foraging for vegetables in June is great! You name it and it's there for the picking, plucking, snipping, snapping or digging.

Lamb's-quarters (*Chenopodium album*) is one early summer potherb that is prized by nearly everyone who tries it. This spinachlike annual, with a whitish granular coating on its leaves, grows along roadsides throughout temperate North America.

My family eagerly awaits our first June dinner of lamb's-quarters. I usually wait until the grayish plants are five or six inches high, then pluck off the tops. Other tops will sprout from the sides of the plant, so topping does not destroy the plant for later cutting. I have gone back to the same weed patch four times during one summer and have even served this topless tender potherb fresh for Thanksgiving.

Lamb's-quarters are easy to gather and contain no grit. The granular consistency of the leaves is removed by rubbing handfuls of the greens together in cold water. I pop the washed plant tops into boiling, salted water, cook five minutes, drain, dot with butter, pepper, salt, and serve. Leftover lamb's-quarters make a splendid salad with vinegar-and-oil dressing, or if you gather too much for one cooking, the fresh greens will keep well in plastic bags in the refrigerator.

Years ago Oriental peoples discovered that our common yard plant daylily (*Hemerocallis fulva*) is one of the most rewarding food plants on earth. In addition to the daylily sprouts, which may be eaten in March, the nearly grown flower buds are ready to pick about the end of June. Because they grow in accessible areas along country lanes and along streams, novices at foraging can spot them and snap off unopened flower buds. We pick daylily buds when they are about one to two inches long, then rinse them and drop them into salted, boiling water for four minutes of cooking. Before dropping them into boiling water, supper should be ready, because their bright-green, crunchy goodness does not hold for any length of time. Daylily buds taste somewhat like fresh green beans, and like the bean, the only way to ruin this simple vegetable is by overcooking.

Daylily buds in sour cream is an interesting variation. Mix together one-quarter cup of mayonnaise, one-half pint of sour cream and two tablespoons of lemon juice. Heat the mixture, but do not boil. Place the cooked, well-drained, hot daylily buds in a casserole and pour the heated sour cream over them. Sprinkle with salt, pepper, paprika and serve immediately.

When vegetable soup is on the menu and daylilies are nodding in the June breeze, dash outside and snap off a handful of the old orange lily heads. Cooked in soup, the wilted daylily flowers add a gelatinous garnish.

I have dried the wilted daylily flowers and stored them in sterilized jars for winter soups. To dry, merely pick the ones that are withered, lay them on wax paper in the sun until dry, give them a ten-minute 180° F. oven treatment and store in a lidded jar.

Gypsies use elder flowers to strengthen their powers, my grandfather used to say each June as we hiked creek banks to gather elder blow. I never asked what powers. I once actually saw a gypsy snipping elder blooms by the gunnysackful. When I asked him why, he swung his black hair from his face and almost hissed:

> *Witches' tree*
> *Witches' tea*
> *Witches will not bother me.*

Thinking back on his hostile, secretive manner, I cannot imagine any witch daring to bother him. To me he was a suspicious, fearful creature, wickedly handsome, swarthy and threatening in an intangible way.

Years later, a more communicative gypsy told me, "The flowers make a creamy tea that is valuable for the lungs. It's a sure cure for colds."

I learned that gypsies quick-dry the full-ripe elder flowers by placing the umbels on screening in a warm, dry place. "Not in the sun nor in a hot oven," she warned. "The sun draws the medicine from the bloom."

The gypsy said they also steeped fresh flowers in boiling water for forty-eight hours and then drained them, fermented the juice and distilled the liquid for use in bronchial and flu medicine, which they sold.

The elder (*Sambucus nigra* or *canadensis*) is a potent patriarch of the plant world. Wherever it grows, elder discourages other herbs. Animals usually don't like the rank elder taste, either.

The elder plant is a large shrub with finely toothed pinnate leaves combining as many as nine leaflets on a stem. Small white flowers cluster at the end of woody stalks and are followed by heavy umbels of blue-black berries. Elder has a noticeable odor when the leaves or stalks are broken. It grows in lowlands and open pastures from Quebec southward, throughout eastern and central United States.

Elderberries and elder blooms have long been popular as a source of wine. Personally I find the blossom wine intriguing. The power of elder-blow wine is difficult to describe. Because of its dirty-foot smell, I call it my footwash. However, after the first sip has deadened one's olfactory glands, no wine is finer.

The creamy elder blow is cut with scissors or snapped off after the sun reaches it but before the bugs get up—bugs do little to enrich the flavor of this wine.

Uncle Steve's elder-blow wine was almost as famous as the Brewster sisters' berry product, but of course he didn't lace his with arsenic. He picked about three-fourths of a bushel of expanded elder flowers and mixed them with twelve pounds of sugar in a ten-gallon crock. Over this he poured five gallons of boiling water, covered it, and let it stand overnight. The next morning he stirred in one package of yeast which had been dissolved in one cup of warm water. This was allowed to ferment for one week and was stirred regularly. The webby, brown mess was then strained and the liquid poured into a keg containing about three pounds of chopped raisins.

Grandaddy bought raisins and prunes in bulk. He put the gooey raisins on a board for me to run through the chopper. He cleaned the meat chopper with a handful of groats, which also went into the wine. The barrel was bunged with a fermentation lock until Christmas, when the wine was tasted, strained a second time and sealed.

Grandaddy often said that elder-blow wine will keep bad witches and evil tongues away from a house, but I cannot vouch for it.

Elder blossoms are also good to eat. Every June, just before supper, I cross the road to the golf course to pluck handfuls of the pale blooms. Back home, I remove the flowers from the heavy stems and drop pinch-sized clusters into a bowl of sweet, ginger-flavored wine. As the elder blooms soak up their last drink, I mix a hot cake batter enriched with an extra egg. Just before sitting down at the table I take a tiny wad of the heady flowers from the wine, drop them into the batter, swish them around to coat them well, then fry them in deep fat until lightly browned. I serve them sprinkled with powdered sugar on a fold of the local paper. Elder fritters are sweet finger food; small kids love them and grown kids lick their fingers and reach for more.

If Grandma had leftover sour-pickle juice, she would blanch unopened elder-flower buds briefly in boiling water (in and out), then pack them into a hot, sterilized jar. She covered them with the boiling pickle juice, sealed them, and used the knobby pickled buds as capers in salads.

My grandfather held strong feelings about elders—both elder plants and elder people. He said that the elder plant had lots to offer man; and he said that elder people had a lot to offer, too. He believed all youths need elders or grandparents to interpret the past. Because grandparents give a family roots, he felt that the isolation of grandparents weakened the second generation of that family. Elder people are the roots of the family as well as the roots of the broader culture, he said. He gave me this lecture every time we went blossom hunting. When we came home he would pour a glass of elder-blow wine and drink a toast to grandparents. All by himself, he'd raise his glass and say, "To elders."

With that annual June toast, I'd see in my mind's eye the heavy, creamy elder umbels bowing before the sun. A moment later I'd visualize a sea of bowed gray heads in church. As my mind conjured up feelings about elders, I felt their powers, I felt the power of maturity in June.

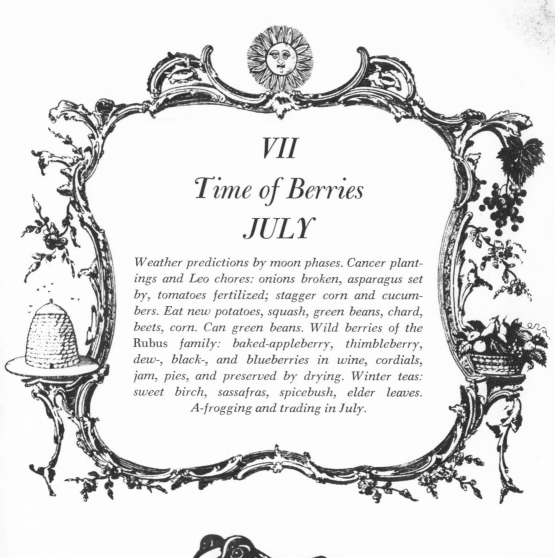

VII
Time of Berries
JULY

Weather predictions by moon phases. Cancer plant-ings and Leo chores: onions broken, asparagus set by, tomatoes fertilized; stagger corn and cucum-bers. Eat new potatoes, squash, green beans, chard, beets, corn. Can green beans. Wild berries of the Rubus family: baked-appleberry, thimbleberry, dew-, black-, and blueberries in wine, cordials, jam, pies, and preserved by drying. Winter teas: sweet birch, sassafras, spicebush, elder leaves. A-frogging and trading in July.

WEATHER, OF COURSE, influences the maturation of plants, and my grandfather often predicted weather by the moon phases. Weather predictions were treated as a sort of game in our family, and all of us watched and joked about the moon.

If the moon's change occurs between:	the weather will be:
midnight and 2:00 A.M.	fair
2:00 and 4:00 A.M.	cool and stormy
4:00 and 8:00 A.M.	wet
8:00 and 12:00 noon	changeable
12:00 noon and 2:00 P.M.	rainy and blustery
2:00 and 4:00 P.M.	mild and showers
4:00 and 8:00 P.M.	fair and windy
8:00 and 10:00 P.M.	clear and colder
10:00 P.M. and midnight	fair

The time of the moon's changes, that is, the new moon, first quarter, full moon and last quarter, are significant points in weather prediction, according to those who predict by the moon.

For weather prognostications over a longer period my grandfather quoted a farmer who traded him grapes for barrels (Grandaddy was a cooper by training). The nearer the moon's change is to midnight, the fairer the weather will be for the following seven days. Conversely, the nearer the moon's change is to noontime, the more foul the weather will be for the next seven days.

Some old-timers believed that if a northwest wind rode in on a new moon, the wind would howl until the change.

One man predicted that if the full moon and equinox met, violent storms would ensue, followed by a dry spring.

Another farmer watched thunderstorms. He believed that thunder at the moon changes meant the weather would be mild and moist, "good for crops," he claimed.

The fruitful, watery, feminine zodiac sign of Cancer extends from June 21 to July 22, and any July planting should be done during this time if the moon phase is right, astrologers advise. Seeds planted under the sign of Cancer will be deep-rooted and will breed true and even. Although they will not produce bumper crops, they will sprout and mature quickly and the fruit will be filled with juice. Cancer plantings do not store well, so the crops must be harvested as soon as they ripen and eaten immediately.

A farmer friend who farms by the zodiac asserts that Cancer-planted horse corn should be fed out before winter and never made into silage or kept in a crib. "She'll mold while you're looking at her," he told me.

The last part of July falls under the old king sign of Leo (July 22 to August 23) and is characterized by fiery, barren, dry and masculine tendencies. Never plant anything during the last week of July. Zodiac followers say you should grub your garden of its last weeds and thin the late crops of beets, parsnips, turnips and rutabagas at this time.

Onion tops falling over indicate that they are ripening. To prevent neck rot, break the onion stalks so they lie horizontally along the ground; then the onions may be harvested when the moon is growing old. The time during the third and fourth quarters of the moon under the sign of Leo was when my grandfather dug onions. They should be dug a week or so after they are broken, and left on the top of the ground in full exposure to the sun for a few days to dry completely, he advised. The onions should then be gathered and the perfect or "keeping" ones should be spread loosely in an airy shelter until stored for the winter.

JULY

Asparagus should be set by, that is, weeded and fertilized for the last time, under the sign of Leo. Asparagus is a heavy feeder, and to insure a vigorous crop for the following spring, it should be fertilized or mulched with compost in July.

Tomatoes should be fertilized in July; like mothers' prenatal vitamins, a shot gives them a boost to produce.

My grandfather "handled" his horseradish each July; that is, he dug down and rubbed off the side roots to encourage one straight horseradish root to form.

Squash are selfish, sociopathic types that need control. Give them an inch and they'll take over the cucumbers. Too chickenhearted to prune, I gently pick up the encroaching tendrils and swing the vine back on itself.

The last staggered planting of corn and cucumbers should be scheduled for early July because the fruit is not likely to mature if planted too late. Some farmers say both corn and cucumbers should be planted during the first quarter of the moon. Planted at that time, the ears of corn will reach outward from the stalk and try to grab the new moon; thus they are more easily fertilized by falling or blowing pollen. If corn is planted during the second quarter of the moon, the ears are said to hang close to the stalk in fear of the larger moon. Thus the corn silk does not catch the pollen and fewer grains will mature.

Fertilization of cucumber flowers by insects is also said to be affected by the moon. When the moon is a new sliver, the bugs rest at night and are vigorous by day. As the nights grow brighter with the waxing moon, fertilizing-type creatures romp all night and are too pooped to pollinate the cucumbers by day. Cucumbers bloom about four weeks after planting; therefore, if planted early in the first quarter of the moon, they will bloom during the following month when insects are most industrious.

July's garden is filled with good things to eat, and July is the time you can sneak a spud. Fresh new potatoes, boiled in their baby skins, drained, salted, peppered, gently mounded

119

on a plate, drizzled with butter and topped with a plop of sour cream, are "a fit bite for any man," my grandfather would say.

As soon as the potato blossoms disappear, most gardeners hill the plants for the last time and dig a few golf-ball-sized goodies.

More than once the kids have kindled the outside fireplace into action and put the kettle on while I ran to the garden to dig a few new potatoes. Fifteen minutes later we were all sitting around the table, our plates crowded with small, mellow, unpeeled spuds.

My family loves meat, but once or twice a week during July, ripe garden vegetables break the meat routine and are eagerly eaten.

A mountainous platterful of fresh summer squash, sliced, salted, dipped in flour and fried until crisp, tastes great. Tender green beans and new potatoes, boiled separately, drained, then tossed together in a bowl with lots of butter, pepper and salt, make a good meal. Swiss chard, popped into boiling water for twenty minutes, drained, then swizzled with drippings and tidbits of ham, is filling, tasty and tender for lunch. Beets, boiled with their skins on, drained, slipped into cold water, peeled, then doused with olive oil, vinegar, pepper and salt, go well with a can of sardines for a quick meal. And if a gardener is very, very lucky, all-the-corn-you-can-eat, ear on ear, heaped into three bowls on the table, becomes a July reality.

When going the vegetable route for supper, the key is timing. Thirty minutes or less from garden to table—and often the vegetables' own sugar goodness cannot be improved except by adding a touch of salt, pepper and plops of butter.

As I race back to the cabin with the vegetables, I often pull a handful of green onions and a crunch of lettuce to go with a brand-new tomato for a garden salad.

Chores for a July garden are mostly maintenance, cultivation and harvesting, with an occasional spray or top dressing of fertilizer.

Potatoes are often set by; that means hilled up for the final time and left to grow fat and mealy.

Beets like the loose life, so their soil should be cultivated fairly regularly to keep them happy. Although they take about two months to mature, beets grow several plants from each fruit and should be thinned after the tiny beets reach eatable size.

Cabbages are big eaters and should be side-dressed with a nitrogen-heavy fertilizer such as chicken droppings before a rain in early summer.

If your green beans "make," the last of July is the best time to can or freeze any surplus. A bushel of beans will can into eighteen or twenty quarts. If we have enough, I usually can about fifty quarts for my family of five. I try to plant beans so that the main crop will mature in July, which enables me to can them before the rush of August preserving. Beans will keep fairly well on the vine for about ten days, which gives adequate time to allow enough to ripen for canning.

I pickle tender string beans by boiling the whole bean pod (ends included) in salted water and, when cooked through, I pack the long beans into sterilized jars. Using a boiled, spiced vinegar or old pickle juice such as dill or hot pepper, I cover the beans and seal them. They are very good.

July is also the month to can tender greens. Although I have not canned chard, kale, mustard, spinach, turnip or beet tops, or wild greens in our home, I washed and "picked over" my weight in them when I was young. Unless you favor happenings at the table, "picking over" is the most important part of preparing greens for canning. I remember a fascinating black worm on my Uncle Ed's plate. I just knew it had come out of the canned kale. I was so aghast at seeing my uncle sprinkle it with pepper, I couldn't open my mouth. Speechless and rigid, I backed away from the table. My chair fell over. My legs flew up chucking Grandaddy's elbow so that his fork jerked upward to jab him in the soft palate. He shouted, Grandma jumped up, and when everything quieted down, Uncle Ed's plate was empty. By then I was so clothed with remorse that I could not tell anyone what had happened. It was I who had "picked over" those greens.

To this day I handle every leaf as an individual and check both sides, but I do not can greens.

Mixed vegetables are good to can for winter soup. Little dibs and dabs of carrots, green beans and corn and a cabbage leaf or onion give a pleasant taste to a frosty-day soup. Such mixed quarts contain low-acid foods and must be processed for the time needed to preserve the vegetable requiring the longest stay in the canner. Corn and peas, in particular, spoil readily, so canning directions or time and temperature charts should be consulted.

Canning is fun. If one day a week can be devoted to canning from mid-July until the first week in September, the chore is done and the rewards linger throughout the winter. Needs are simple: a large canner kettle with rack and cover, jars and their lids. The initial cost of jars may seem high, but if the jars are washed and stored, the expense can be prorated over ten or more years. Then the only costs involved are lids. The sense of satisfaction and the convenience of having a variety of foods in the basement are the big payoffs to canning. Also, if you suffer from insecurity, you can look at your canned goods from time to time and be reassured.

Abundant July wild foods promote a more immediate sense of security as berries ripen in every glen and meadow.

Over the years I have sought various members of the *Rubus*, blackberry-dewberry family. Most are familiar and eagerly gathered, but one *Rubus* remains somewhat neglected. The baked-appleberry (*Rubus chamaemorus*), or cloudberry, grows in wet areas and in acid peats from the arctic regions southward throughout New England. A single, soft, pinkish berry, the baked-apple grows on a twelve-inch stem which also bears a few scalloped leaves. They are excellent as a fresh dessert, preserved in jams, or prepared as juice. I have heard men praise baked-appleberry pie, but I thought it lacked personality. Cooked, the luscious cloudberry faces an identity crisis; eaten raw or made into jam, it is great. Many northland trails are well-beaten paths through cloudberry patches where it is possible to drop your hands, open your fingers and scoop handfuls of nourishment without missing a step.

The thimbleberry (*Rubus parviflorus*) is another northern fruit. It has plump elongated berries that are excellent fresh, preserved or used in drinks.

My mental berry calendar marks July Fourth as Dewberry Day, and Bastille Day for blackberries in Virginia. Dewberries of the *Rubus* family grow on trailing vines throughout pine woods and are often found creeping along the ground. Blackberries (two hundred *Rubus* species) may be high or low bush but are always very stickery. Dewberries are often less acrid than their black cousins and seem to be consistently larger, too. However, we have some patches of blackberries as big as a man's thumb that grow along the stream banks and in moist spring weeps. When late frosts wipe out exposed blackberries, the creeping dewberry holds up the *Rubus* family honor because it is less vulnerable under the trees. There is rarely a *Rubus*-less year. Most recipes that call for blackberries may be used interchangeably with dew- or raspberries, thimble-, baked-apple-, or their western friends, the loganberries or salmonberries.

Blackberry wine, or wine made from any of the *Rubus* cousins, develops the strong color and character of port. Berries for wine, if picked after the sun or air has dried the morning dew, will ferment naturally, with little or no encouragement; however, I usually play it safe by adding yeast to my brew. Anything that is black, shiny and doesn't move I pop into my bucket, and when I have two gallons of berries I mash them in a plastic bucket and pour five quarts of boiling water over them. I cover the bucket and put it in a cool, dark place. A day or so later I dissolve twelve cups of sugar in one gallon of boiling water and after cooling the syrup to luke-warm, I mix it with the crushed berries and add one package of dry yeast dissolved in warm water. The wine is allowed to ferment in a covered container for two weeks. I usually cover it with plastic wrapping held in place by an elastic garter which facilitates the cover removal for frequent stirring. I strain the wine after fermentation has slowed, let it settle, and in one or two days I siphon it into sterilized bottles, cap lightly, and when all action has stopped I pound the corks home and seal each bottle with paraffin. This deep-bodied wine is a sweet-to-dry drink that satisfies.

Simple wine is fun to make; cordials and brandies are tricky. For a counterfeit cordial that is foolproof and superior to sip, mash three quarts of blackberries through a jelly sack, add two cups of sugar to every two cups of juice and stir until dissolved. Cover and let stand in a cool, dark place for three or four days. Add the clear, sweet juice to cheap brandy and the result is a fresh-fruit-flavored, rich and pleasant cordial. Part of the fun is in testing your mixture to determine the exact proportions you desire. You should do this with your husband or a good friend.

My grandmother used to say that two or three doses of blackberry cordial would check diarrhea and arrest dysen-tery, but I have not served it with that in mind. Poured over slivered ice it makes a fine drink.

Rivaling blackberry wine in popularity is berry jam. The basic rule of successful jam or jelly making is: *Work with small quantities*.

My basic recipe for making berry jam is: Wash and crush four cups of berries, mix in three cups of sugar, and boil slowly in a *large*, heavy pot for ten minutes while washing and sterilizing jars.

The water content of berries affects the jellying point so the exact cooking time cannot be calculated. I use the eyeball method. Jams and jellies boil high on the pan, and when they start boiling down (that is when you can see one-quarter inch or so distance between the boiling surface and the high mark on the side of the pot, where the liquid has been), start testing for the jellying point. To test for the jellying point, dip a spoon into the boiling jam or syrup. Tilt the spoon until the liquid runs off. Watch the drips. When the jellying point is reached, the last two drops will run together, then flake, or sort of skid from the spoon.

When the jellying point is reached, remove the jam from the fire, and immediately pour the hot liquid into hot jelly jars. While the jam is still warm, seal with vacuum caps or paraffin.

I use the basic recipe, four to three, fruit to sugar, with most berries, pulp or juice.

Lewis braves the brambles with me each year in exchange for promises of blackberry pies. Two or three cups of washed berries are half crushed with three-fourths cup of sugar that has been previously mixed with two tablespoons of flour and a pinch of salt. They are poured into an unbaked pie shell and topped with a crust, which is perforated, sealed and baked at 425° F. for forty-five minutes.

The hundreds of species of *Rubus* are July's gifts to man. They may be nibbled in the field, stewed, jellied, jammed, juiced, pickled, pied, preserved, cobbled, canned and dried.

Indians of the north country dry blackberries into a pemmican cake for winter food. Some preserve them in fats, then mix them with snow for arctic ice cream.

Drying is the simplest and cheapest manner of preserving berries. Handled properly, they will keep a superior flavor. Reconstituted dry berries may be substituted for canned fruit in pies, shortcakes and sauces. Cleanliness is the key to successful drying. Freedom from dirt and insects during drying is very important.

To dry berries, use firm, nearly ripe but not mushy, fruit; do not wash berries. Put them one layer thick into an oven and thoroughly heat them at 150° F. for about twenty minutes. Do not hold them in the oven long enough to cook them. When heated sufficiently to kill undesirable bacteria, spread the berries in the sun to dry. They should be spread thinly on enamel, wood or stone and covered with netting. Take the berries inside at night to prevent sweating. Ten days of good sunlight should dry most berries; however, the species and size will alter the time required. I have dried raspberries in three days of hot sun after an oven treatment.

The dried berries should be stored in sterilized, covered jars, which may, but need not be, vacuum sealed. When reconstituted with water, by soaking overnight or gently boiling for thirty minutes, a little sugar and a wee sprinkle of salt seems to bring them to life.

I regularly can blackberries to be used as a breakfast fruit or in pies. One quart of drained berries makes a fine pie plus a sampling of juice for the kids. To can blackberries or any of the *Rubus* friends, I wash, drain and measure. For each quart of berries I gently mix in one-quarter cup of sugar. Some berries will mash and make a little juice. When the mixture is all beautifully red, I heat them slowly and boil them until the sugar has dissolved. I spoon the hot berries and their syrup into hot, sterilized jars, cover them with juice and a little boiling water, enough to bring the contents one-half inch from the top of the jar. The jars are sealed and the quarts processed for thirty minutes in a boiling-water bath.

Heaped over pistachio ice cream, these somewhat tart berries are a snappy dessert.

Your berry eye has not completed its July work until blueberries and whortleberries are gathered. True blueberries (*Vaccinium*) bear their fruit in terminal clusters and grow in eastern North America, while whorts are borne in the leaf axils and are found across the northern United States. Both blueberries and whortleberries have many soft seeds and thrive in somewhat dry, open areas. Both are blue, black or purplish, with a bloom.

JULY

My grandfather, working as a fireman, kept a mental log of local woods fires. After a year or so he'd scout the burned-over areas for huckleberries, because he said they produced more fruit after a fire. Although he lumped huckleberries, whorts and blueberries under the same name, true huckle-berries (*Gaylussacia*) have larger seeds and a waxiness on both leaves and new shoots. I do not remember which kind we picked in Missouri. They all taste similar but specific areas produce distinctively flavored berries.

Some people pick blueberries by the fistful, but our berries in Virginia are so skimpy we pick them one at a time and feel ourselves lucky if we get a cupful for a batch of muffins. Our daughter, Marie, makes a wicked muffin with our precious blueberries. The clue, she tells me, is to mix the shortening and moist ingredients first, dump the sifted dry ingredients into the bowl next, and pour the blueberries on top of the flour mixture. Mix only until the berries are coated and the flour is moist. She bakes them in a hot oven for fifteen or twenty minutes while she crisp-fries bacon and heats a bowl of beans. For a Sunday-night supper, beans, bacon, and blueberry muffins are hard to beat.

In addition to the wild berries we enjoyed, Grandaddy's perennial garden contained a variety of "boughten" berries. My favorite was the lowly gooseberry (*Ribes*), whose prickly, sour fruit baked into a tangy pie. Gooseberry pie is still my favorite, although we do not grow gooseberries in Virginia because they are associated with a rust disease of pine. After we planted our eroded gullies with thousands of baby pines, parenthood with all its pride and agony took over, and any threat to offspring was avoided even if it meant giving up rich, tart, puckery-sweet gooseberry pies.

In addition to winter stores of berries and beans, leaves for many winter beverages are gathered during July.

Though not as bracing as India teas, wild teas are pleasant and refreshing. While some authorities maintain that most wild teas may be cured by simply drying young, mature leaves in the shade, my grandmother dipped branches of fresh leaves into boiling water for a moment before drying them in a gentle heat. If the day was rainy, she dried tea in the attic; if it was clear, the screens of leaves were brought to the wisteria arbor. They usually dried in a week. The tea was stored by crumpling the dried leaves into sterilized, dry pint jars, which were then capped.

I have used the quick-boiling dip, then dried twigs and leaves of sweet birch (*Betula lenta*), which brews into a warming beverage that hints of wintergreen and pleasant summer hikes.

Sassafras (*Sassafras albidum*) roots and leaves brewed fresh or dried give a flavorful and colorful tea. Insipidly root-beerish on first taste, this beverage grows on you until the merest suggestion of its aromatic odor whets the appetite for sassy-tea. I use cream and sugar in my tea, and like the lady who gets three or four "trips" to a tea bag, I brew roots over and over until the flavor is gone.

Spicebush tea (*Lindera benzoin*) is another fragrant caffeine-free winter drink made from dried and crumbled twigs and leaves. The river near our cabin is bordered with spice-bush and, though the shrub is reputed to be non-narcotic, the mockingbirds have a ball as they light, nibble a red berry, flutter aloft, and return for another. Some year I am going to dry and powder the berries, which traditionally are supposed to be a substitute for allspice. I can see it now, my guests fluttering aloft after nibbles on my Snappy Ding-a-lings (allspice cookies).

Young wild-strawberry-leaf tea (*Fragaria virginiana*) and blackberry-leaf tea (*Rubus* family) were a disappointment. My husband said "*Yack!*" The taste did resemble the smell of last year's hay. Recently I learned that I should add dried orange peeling to brew a tasty strawberry-leaf tea, but I may not have the courage to serve it again.

Care should be taken not to collect leaves of raspberries

(*Rubus occidentalis*) for tea because they are said to be poisonous if dried during some stages of development.

I have been tempted to taste white-clover tea (*Trifolium repens*) because the dried flowers smell so good. But it would be just my luck to end up with bloat. I once saw a poor cow lying head downhill with a two-by-four between her jaws and a cow doctor pressing on her belly. How she moaned and rolled her eyes! I'd hate to have that happen to me. The farmer said she had eaten too much white clover.

Members of the *Ilex* family—yaupon (*Ilex vomitoria*), inkberry (*I. glabra*) (not pokeweed, commonly called inkberry), holly (*I. Opaca*) and black alder (*I. laevigata*) are also said to be substitutes for caffeine-free tea.

My favorite wild tea is brewed from dried elder leaves (*Sambucus canadensis*). Surprisingly sweet, pale in color, but robust in flavor, elder tea needs no additive for complete satisfaction. I full-boil the leaves about one minute, let them steep for about three minutes, then strain and drink.

Grandaddy liked to search creek banks on July evenings and pick a bag of elder leaves for tea; then we'd go a-frogging. Although in some areas night hunting of bullfrogs is outlawed, I remember with equal emotion the sport and the delicate taste of frogs' legs.

Just before dusk my grandfather would load his fishing gear, flashlights, a lunch and me into the Essex and head for the flats where numerous creeks meandered to the Missouri. With me wearing old sneakers, because Grandma said a girl's feet would spread if not shod, we first picked leaves from the spooky, droopy elder bushes; then I followed my grandfather into the black water. He knew all the creeks and the favored hangouts of the local frogs. Each of us holding a light in one hand and a stout pole in the other, we waded as silently as possible to the center of the stream. I always giggled nervously at the squishy mud and the feel of cool water lapping my legs. There is a nearness to nature when prowling in a shallow stream on a dark, warm night; the creak of insects, the suck of water, the droning of mosquitoes, peepers, amorous frogs all weave a noisy web about the sleepy earth. There is a tinge of fear, too.

Uncle Steve's frog gun was famous throughout St. Joseph. To the end of a pole he tied a fishing line. On the bottom of the string, which was an arm's length longer than the pole, he fastened a three-pronged hook. Six to eight inches above the hook he tied a tiny bit of red flannel.

Moving noiselessly upstream, our flashlights probing the undercut banks with light, we peered and stalked. Our right hands held the poles and dangling hooks. If there was bank brush, we raised the pole overhead because nothing was as frustrating as a caught hook in the dark. It was practically impossible to hold the light and free the hook at the same time.

Bullfrogs like to serenade their sweethearts under remote rooty banks. When we spotted proper-sized frog's eyes reflecting like green-glass beads, all motion stopped. The idea was to hold the light steadily on the frog and carefully manipulate the red flannel to a position directly in front of and above the frog's head. This was tricky because depth perception at night was distorted and squiggly light trails on the water confused the distance factor even further. The frog usually continued to sing his heart out as the red flag moved closer and closer. Slowly and smoothly the flannel had to be positioned so that the frog would raise his head to watch it. At the moment when the frog's bulging eyes seemed to point skyward as if in prayer, the hook was leveled under his upraised chin, jerked and impaled in the bullfrog's jaw. If the hook was positioned correctly there was no splash or fight. I have seen my grandfather lift a frog from under a bank with a jerk so precise that its outstretched seven-inch legs barely skimmed the water, and the frog was removed from the hook and thrust into a gunnysack without a whisper of noise. I always seemed to hook my frog in the gullet or some other awkward place so that the poor thing splashed into the water and created such a rumpus that all bullfrogs within a half-mile radius took flight. Also, I never learned to remove a frog from the hook. It is a wonder that my grandfather had enough patience to take me frogging with him.

Even working quietly, we had to stand still for a moment or two to "let nature come back" after the hush that fell over the flatland when a creature was caught. We worked upstream and then down, illuminating the water-level mark on the banks in our search for bullfrog eyes.

Skinning a frog sounds unsavory, but actually it is a simple and not unpleasant task. After the throat is slit, the frog is held by one leg with the left hand and dipped into running water, then the leg by which the frog is held is severed from the body. The frog's weight holds the skin taut and outlines the big leg muscles, making the cutting easy. The knife is laid down and with the right hand the leg skin is slipped backward from the meaty thigh section, like taking off a glove wrong side out. Finally the cleaned leg is placed on a board and the foot end, with the wrong-side-out skin attached, is cut off. Usually no part of the frog except the leg is skinned, and there is little blood or smell. Catch your bullfrog, slit, sever one leg, slip the skin back, cut at the hock, sever the second leg, slip the skin and cut it away with the foot; only pink, clean meat remains.

As part of his fishing gear my grandfather carried an empty beer bucket (a half-gallon container with a tight lid) in which he laid the cleaned frogs' legs for Grandma to fry like chicken when we got home. He liked to clean his meat or fish on the creek bank, because throwing the offal back into the water helped to sustain the balance of wildlife. "I trade with the creek," he declared. "Other creatures' food for frogs' legs." He believed that the earth was a gigantic balance, that when you used one resource you were obligated to trade back to the earth in another way.

His philosophy of "What you got to trade?" related to all phases of life. He would wax poetic on mankind's trade and balance. He was sure that when a man had nothing to trade, that man was doomed. In our times, he said, the old and the young often have relatively little to trade; thus they have a hard time. "You got to have something to trade, either with the earth or with other people," he told me over and over.

I have thought of his words, most especially on humid July days when I'm picking berries and leaves. I am trading with the earth, I say to myself, I trade her fruits for a pledge to protect one tiny square of her wilderness.

VIII
The Beautiful World of Fruit
AUGUST

Lunar gardening. Under Leo, dry and can, pickle and brine: sauerkraut, dry corn, potted corn, hominy. Applesauce and skin wine, fried apples. Peaches brandied, candied and canned. Plums in kuchen and preserves. Wild foods: groundnuts, mayapples in jam, fox grapes in jam, pawpaw bread; and elderberries, canned, dried, fritters and wine. Milkweed pods and puffballs. Iced teas: birch, sumac, mint and nettle. Root beer. Contemplating the earth's goodness on an August afternoon.

PEOPLE WHO garden by the moon consider timing and rhythm extremely important for successful crops. The time of planting, cultivating, eradication of pests and weeds, and the time of harvesting all fall within the rhythm of the moon's phase and the moon's zodiac sign. They believe that an optimum time for every chore exists within the lunar year. Moon-sign followers say that a counterpoint zodiac rhythm exists in the daily moon place sign and that by working in accordance with the sign, phase and daily place sign, a balance with nature is achieved.

Leo (July 22 to August 23) is said to be the most lofty, firm and steadfast of zodiac-gardening signs. Astrologers say that crops harvested under the fiery, barren, dry, masculine characteristics of Leo keep better and longer.

Grains, beans and herbs to be dried should be gathered and prepared for storage under Leo and during the moon's last quarter.

If possible, canning should be done during the dry zodiac sign of Leo. Pickles should be pickled and cabbage krauted under Leo for a firm and zesty product.

My grandfather used to harvest cabbage for kraut just before the full moon because he claimed that this encourages the fermentation process. I have not experienced difficulty with cabbage fermenting at any time; in fact, the whole neighborhood is aware when our kraut is working. Fermenting kraut gives off some provocative odors, but good sauerkraut is worth the stink.

An August garden is all gravy. Lima beans come in, corn is ripe, beets grow into perfect ruby globes, pole beans hang stringless and unashamed, Brussels sprouts sprout, chard is lovely, carrots are in the ground if you didn't thin too thinly, cucumbers beg you to pick them, cantaloupes shape up, squash linger shyly beneath their leaves, pumpkins begin to look like pumpkins, okra pods form, tomatoes are all over the place and cabbage runs rampant.

Cabbage means kraut, kraut means neckbones, ribs, frankfurters and all manner of good meals.

Sauerkraut is shredded cabbage that has been fermented and pickled in brine.

When I make sauerkraut, I remove the green leaves from the cabbage and, with shredder or grater, I slice each head fine. This is easily done by quartering the head and holding the core while you grate.

Although some people wash the shredded cabbage and shake it out, I usually mix unwashed, chopped cabbage with salt and layer it into a crock which has been lined with grape leaves. Grape leaves are said to firm kraut and add bacteria for fermentation. I sometimes sprinkle a bit more salt between handfuls of the salted cabbage. I cover the kraut with grape leaves and then with a wooden lid that fits inside the crock, and finally top everything with a stone to keep the cabbage immersed in brine, and then with a cheesecloth covering. I once used a dinner plate to hold the cabbage in place, but the plate absorbed the brine and still smells like kraut when it is heated.

As the salt draws juice from the cabbage, a liquid will form and cover the lid. This must be skimmed from time to time. If too little brine forms, I add salted water, two tablespoons to the quart of water. The crock should be kept in a cool airy place like behind the big chair in our dining room. When it begins to ripen, smile innocently at people who ask if a mouse has died in your walls.

In about three or four weeks, or when no more foam appears on the brine, the sauerkraut is ready to eat or to can. I can cured kraut when it is white-yellow and free from white-white spots.

I heat it, pack it hot into hot, sterilized quart jars, and if there is not enough juice to cover it, I add a holding brine made by dissolving two tablespoons of plain salt in a quart of boiling water. I process quarts in a boiling-water bath for thirty minutes after each jar has been lidded and sealed.

If I remember, I put a fresh grape leaf into the bottom of each quart. My grandmother canned some of her kraut with caraway seeds, a pinch into the top of each quart. Some people strew juniper berries in their sauerkraut; for me, juniper makes the kraut taste like a hot martini.

Rule of thumb on the amount of salt needed for sauerkraut is about one to one-and-a-half cups of salt for each forty to fifty pounds of cabbage. Plain salt instead of iodized salt is advised.

In addition to putting down kraut early each August, my grandmother used to dry corn for keeping. To dry sweet corn she picked ripe, full ears, removed the husks and silk and cleaned any bad spots. Holding the ears by the stalk end, she plunged each one into unsalted, briskly boiling water. This was an in-and-out operation; she did not let go of the corn. With the tip of the ear pressed against a board she cut the kernels from the cob in one downward stroke, trying to cut as close to the cob as possible in order to have full kernels for drying. The ear was turned and cut until all of the corn was removed.

Working with small quantities, a quart or two at a time, she spread the corn one layer deep on white butcher's paper and put it in the sun. Birds, insects and varmints signaled each other and held annual reunions at corn-drying time, and Grandma's hardest work in drying was running in and out of the house with a broom. Often she stationed me on scarecrow duty. At night she brought the corn into the house.

About three days of sunlight removed most of the moisture and "set the sugar." The papers of corn were brought to the attic, where they were laid out to complete their cure. When thoroughly dry, the corn was stored in sterilized jars with tight lids.

For winter use the dried corn was soaked overnight, then cooked.

Grandma always said she had no luck canning corn because "it went to ferment." Grandaddy commented that in view of his winemaking operation the house was full of ferment and the poor corn didn't know what she expected of it.

Grandma did, however, can corn with tomatoes; this was good in stews, scallops and soup.

When I mention potted corn, eyebrows are raised. Corn put down in salt used to be called "potted." Corn on the cob was boiled fifteen or twenty minutes before the kernels were cut from the cob. The cut-off corn was dried on paper for a few moments, then a one-inch layer of corn was sprinkled into a widemouthed crock, followed by one-half inch of non-iodized salt, another layer of corn and salt, and so on until the jar was filled. The top layer was salt. Melted lard was poured over the whole thing and a cloth was tied across the mouth after the lard hardened. The potted corn was kept in the cool, dry root cellar until we wanted some; then the lard was scooped away, enough corn for a meal was removed, and the lard pressed back into place.

This corn had to be soaked overnight to remove the salt, and when properly leached it became fresh and sweet. I believe it retained corn-on-the-cob flavor better than the dried corn did, although both were tougher than fresh corn, and both were unique.

My grandfather made hominy by dipping dry field corn into a lye solution to remove the skins. But when seven hens died a horrible death after accidentally eating the skins, we didn't make hominy any more. Actually this was a family crisis. The hens started flying around with their necks stretched out like geese. My grandfather tried to catch them, and when he couldn't, he called Grandma. She gave him the dickens all the while the two of them were skithering after hens in the chicken yard. We didn't mention hominy in our house for some years after that.

Besides the multitude of garden vegetables to be harvested, dried or canned in Leo's reign, many fruits come into maturity during August.

Apples have played a significant role in our family life since we moved to northern Virginia. Our Culpeper County ranch is located on the Piedmont, the edge of the apple country.

August and applesauce mingle in my mind as a tart-sweet memory. The season's first apples steamed smooth into plops of rich sauce, served with crunchy johnnycake, create a superbly simple summer supper.

I usually put up several bushels of apples into applesauce because my family enjoys it for any meal. We call it a vegetable, a fruit, a dessert or a salad; wherever applesauce fits on the menu, that is what we name it.

Applesauce is good for cakes and cookies. I have added it to Christmas fruitcakes and have stretched mincemeat pie filling by slipping in a cupful. Babies love it; invalids can eat it; most children like it too. I had a young neighbor boy who came "to visit" when he smelled my applesauce cooking in August. I have seen him eat a quart on one visit. I love to see people eat!

After I can the sauce I make a pale wine from summer-apple peelings and cores.

One extra step that modern-day cautions dictate is: *Wash* the apples thoroughly because of poison sprays. When I am going to make apple-skin wine, I wash the apples before peeling them for sauce. I set the peelings aside with all cores that do not have rot, and after the applesauce is canned, I put down a batch of skin wine.

To the peelings and cores from a bushel of washed apples, I add ten pounds of sugar and four gallons of water and just bring them to a boil. Ten ginger roots are placed on a board, a small group at a time, and with the meat cleaver flat, I bruise the ginger by striking the cleaver with the rolling pin. The beat-up ginger root is then placed in a small cotton bag and put in with the apple peelings. (Do not boil the apple peelings or you will end up with jelly.) I let the wine makings cool, remove the ginger bag, strain the skins through a cloth and add to the liquid remaining a cake of yeast which has been dissolved in a cup of warm water and a teaspoon of sugar. I then put the ginger bag back into the apple liquid, cover it and let it work in a cool place for two weeks. The juice must be strained, settled and siphoned into sterilized bottles. Drop a few chunks of the bruised ginger root into each bottle and cork lightly. After it has finished working and the corks stay down, bung them home and seal with paraffin.

Skin wine, served cold over ice, or mulled with spices for a winter drink, is pleasant; like a bowl of applesauce, it satisfies.

Fresh fried summer apples are another food ranked *EEE* (Excellent Everyday Eating).

I do not peel fried apples. I wash, quarter, core and slice them into a mixing bowl of water. While I am fixing the five or six apples for frying, I heat some bacon, sausage or ham. When the meat is almost done I remove it from the skillet and save two tablespoons of grease in the pan for frying the apples. (Sometimes I fry apples in straight butter.) Using my hands as a strainer, I slop the sliced apples from their bowl into the skillet and cover them. This helps steam the apples for quick cooking. When the apples are nearly done, in about ten minutes, I remove the lid, let the remaining water dissipate, and at the last moment before serving sprinkle them with one-half cup of sugar and one teaspoon of cinnamon. Also at the last minute, I finish frying the meat and serve the two together. We all enjoy fried apples. They take about twenty minutes from tree to table; they smell good, look good and are good.

AUGUST

Peaches, without a doubt, are unsurpassed as our favorite, and the middle of August is the time to sharpen our peach tasters. Tree ripened, oozing flavor and juice, richly colored, peaches are superior eaten raw, sliced with cream, pickled, pied, jammed or canned, cobbled, made into ice cream, candied and brandied.

I have a brandied-peaches trick that produces a sweet liqueur as well as a sweetmeat that adds flair to any meal.

Wash, drain, and sort firm-ripe small clingstone or undersized white peaches. Put the fruits into a wire basket or cheesecloth and dip them into boiling water for a minute to loosen their skins. Pop the peaches into cold water and drain. Peel or slip off the skins. If the peaches are clingstones they should be processed whole; if they are freestone, cut them into halves and pit them.

Drop the peeled fruit into a quart or half-gallon jar, alternating one layer of peaches, one layer of sugar, until level full, making sure that the topmost layer is sugar.

Using wine that lacks personality, pour it over the peaches to fill all the cracks between the peaches and the sugar. The wine will weep to the bottom of the jar, moistening the sugar and outlining distinct peach and sugar layers.

Screw on a porcelain or plastic-lined lid (metal darkens fruit) and store the jars in a dark place until early winter.

Before the holidays, check the brandied peaches. If there is no sign of granulated sugar, the peaches and brandy are ready to eat.

Served in an heirloom cut-glass bowl and garnished with greenery, the golden brandied peaches make a showy and delicious accent for pallid or leftover meats.

We have a friend who enjoys the peach brandy drizzled over chipped ice while sitting by his pool on a warm summer night.

I candy peaches by slicing the peeled peaches thinly and boiling them until clear in a syrup made of half their weight in sugar. I then lay the slices on dishes in the sun and turn

141

them every day for about five days until dry. They may be eaten immediately as a confection or packed in jars with powdered sugar over each layer. The chief problem in sun candying is keeping the fruit free from moisture and bugs. I also have trouble keeping little fingers out of these candies; they are delicious.

Peach preserves may be flavored with a cracked pit, maraschino cherries, lemon, almond extract or spices; however, my family enjoys peach preserves plain.

Canned peaches served with sponge cake make a convenient dessert for supper and, like applesauce, may be converted into a toothsome breakfast fruit or a dainty luncheon salad. Our family loves to can peaches. We can them in the country over an open fire, and once in production, we put up fifty jars in a day.

I have made wine out of the skins of peaches, but because I am fearful of modern insecticides, I have discontinued the operation.

My grandmother spiced peaches by inserting into each peach, which had been washed and rubbed free of fuzz, a whole clove and a wedge of stick cinnamon. She filled a two-gallon crock with the peaches and then covered them with boiling sweet-pickle juice made of two quarts of wine vinegar, fifteen pounds of sugar and a cup of pickling spices. The spices, equal parts cinnamon, ginger, cloves and allspice, had first been placed in a sack and boiled in the vinegar for one-half hour. Each day for a week Grandma drained the pickle juice off the peaches, heated it to boiling and returned it to the peach crock. At the end of a week, she heated the peaches in their spice syrup and packed them hot into hot, sterilized jars, covered them with their boiling pickle juice and sealed them.

Spiced peaches turn a pretty amber, and six or eight quarts make a pleasant variation with chicken or mutton for winter dinners.

Unfortunately, plums have gone the commercialized "Eat

me only fresh, fresh, fresh!" route, and those places that still serve cooked plums seem to give them second-class status.

Plums may be preserved, made into butter, baked into puddings and cakes, boiled, pickled and whipped into a scrumptious ice cream. And every chance we get, we make a plum kuchen, introduced to us by a German neighbor lady.

Cream one-half stick of butter with three-fourths cup of sugar. Add one egg, one teaspoon of vanilla, then alternate one-and-three-fourths cup of flour and three-fourths cup of milk a little at a time into the mixture, adding three teaspoons of baking powder and one-half teaspoon of salt. Beat until smooth. Pour into a greased pan, dust with a handful of bread crumbs and lay one pound of pitted plums on top. Bake at 350° F. for thirty-five minutes and, when almost done, sprinkle the surface with two tablespoons of granulated sugar. Serve hot. *Der Kuchen* is delicious.

Tart blue, yellow or red plums may be used in kuchen, but we save damsons for jam. Damsons boil into the finest jam ever piled on crackers. Simple to make, too.

First harness the kids in front of the TV and get them to pit the plums.

Weigh the fruit. Mix in equal pounds of sugar and let stand for four hours.

If you use two pounds of fruit and two pounds of sugar, add one cup of water. Boil, watching the mixture and stirring often. The plums will get glassy and the mixture will be very dry for jam. When it almost reaches the jellying point, that is, when the juice flakes off the spoon and the plum pieces don't want to move, remove the pot from the heat, pour the jam into hot, sterile jars and seal.

One last honorable disposal of plums, which I have not attempted, is brandy. A mountain man uses local wild plums as a ferment, and after several supersecret steps, he reputedly ages his plum juice by tying a keg of it under a certain rocking plank on a wooden bridge. When my husband and I were picking some miniature amber plums with the idea of making a blushing plum butter, we met the plum-brandy man. He showed us where more fruit grew, and in spite of the sticky work and humid August heat, we enjoyed the afternoon foraging with a pro. When we had enough for our needs, we asked the old-timer if we could give him a lift home. He accepted, saying that his feet were much abused since "they" took his truck.

"Who took your truck?" my husband asked.

"Revenuers," he answered positively.

"How did you know it was the revenuers who took it?"

"They took me, too," the old man said with a glint in his eye.

It seems he stopped on the bridge and went below with a companion to sample the brandy. Several other cars drove up, and acquaintances joined them. Someone brought a guitar, a couple of guns were produced for a shooting match, and by nightfall the place was rocking. "Must have been seven or ten cars on the bridge when they drove up and took my truck," he told us.

When we were picking plums with him, his case had not yet come to trial; we have since learned that the charges against him were dropped. Once in a while we see him chugging along country lanes in his pickup, and we wonder what plum patch he's raiding. One of these days, however, when we see his tattered truck parked on a wooden bridge we intend to stop and talk plums.

Uncle Steve used to advise that August is the time to hunt with your nose. Fortunately you don't need his, or my, generous proboscis to sniff out food. Anyone with ordinary olfactory glands can smell groundnut flowers or ripe mayapples a quarter of a mile away.

Groundnut plants, or Indian potatoes (*Apios americana*), should be identified in August when they bloom. The chocolate-purple pealike groundnut flowers have a potent, heavy, sweet fragrance and are difficult to see because their darkness blends into shadowy thickets, but their overpowering scent in August is a dead giveaway.

I have found groundnut vines smothering lowland shrubbery along stream beds and I found one in my tomato-seedling box on my dining-room windowsill. I had unknowingly gathered a groundnut with my potting soil, and the fragile vine grew to the ceiling and now trails along the drapery rod.

The flowering groundnuts are marked in August, but they are not dug until fall when their tubers are full.

Apios americana grow two or three inches below the surface of the ground and several tuber roots grow under each plant on a root string. Though my grandfather did not dig deeply, he had to turn over several square feet of soil to locate the nuts, and it took him about an hour to dig a bucketful. The narrow oval leaflets of the groundnut vine are similar to bean leaves but have five or seven leaflets instead of three; groundnut-bean pods are one to two inches long and grow sparsely on the delicate vines.

My Grandmother used to wash, slice and fry groundnuts in their jackets. Though they are mealy, like white potatoes, they have a mild turnipy taste. I have boiled groundnuts, then swished them around in drippings before serving. The Indians roasted them.

A member of the barberry family, mayapple, or wild lemon (*Podophyllum peltatum*), hides its virtue under an umbrella. Sometimes mayapple plants have only one large, deeply divided leaf with the stem attached to the center. More often they have two umbrella leaves about eight inches in diameter, cut by deep clefts. The single waxy white flower, snuggling against the center stalk under the leaf, blooms in May; it soon withers and a lemonlike berry or fruit the size of a pullet egg forms.

In August the ripe fruit is reminiscent of papaya in taste and consistency, and rather cloying when eaten raw. This may be your taster tricking you, because since mayapples smell like lemons, tartness is anticipated and the sweet, passionless fruit is a disappointment.

Mayapples when cooked lose their suggestion of lemon but take on a distinctive cranberry tartness and boil into pleasantly smooth jam. Simmer three quarts of stemmed, cut-up mayapples in one cup of water for about thirty minutes, stirring every so often, and when they are mushy put them through a colander and set the pulp aside.

Boil three quarts of whole crab apples, either thumbnail-sized flowering crabs or conventional fruit, in water to cover for thirty minutes. Cool, drain through a jelly sack, squeeze all the gooey juice from them by twisting the sack. To every two cups of mayapple pulp add two cups of crab-apple juice, one finely chopped whole lemon and three cups of sugar.

Boil the mixture lustily for twenty minutes, watching for it to start boiling down. When the surface level of the boiling pulp is about one-quarter of an inch from its high mark on the side of the pan, start testing for thickness. Stir it constantly, turn down the fire and do not take your eyeballs from it.

The color will become a golden sardonyx and the pulpy jam will plop and spat little bursts of steam that smell lemony. When the jam reaches the desired thickness, boil it one more minute, stirring continuously; take it off the fire and pour it into hot, sterilized jars. Seal with paraffin or with vacuum caps.

Mayapple jam is a magical concoction that breathes thoughts of deep rich woods and wee elfmen marching under tattered green umbrella leaves. It spreads smoothly on hot bread or tender, thin crackers.

A third nose-twisting August happiness is the fox grape (*Vitis labrusca*). Large as Concords and not unlike Concord grapes in flavor, wild fox grapes grow best in moist bottom land and often climb high in trees. They form four or five grape clusters and are reddish blue to purple when ripe. Their bloom is not pronounced. Their leaves are large, thick and distinctly lobed. All little creatures, especially grouse, are fond of them. I once saw two grouse walk through a low-hanging grape patch and literally strip it of fruit.

Fox grapes are excellent to eat raw, and they make fine wine, juice, grape catsup, marmalade and jelly.

Our daughter Penny makes fox-grape jam by boiling the stemmed grapes for about fifteen minutes in just enough water to keep them from sticking. When they are cooked into a brilliant red and seedy mash, she cools them, squeezes them through a jelly sack, and to every four cups of pulpy juice extracted she adds three cups of sugar. Penny boils her grape jam in a large heavy pot until the jellying point is reached, removes it from the heat and pours it into hot, sterilized jars for sealing with paraffin. She saved a cup of her first effort for her daddy's breakfast and he pronounced it the best fox-grape jam that ever smothered hot buttered toast. Its flavor is intense, tart yet intriguingly sweet.

Since moving to the Washington suburbs, we often visit the Calvert Cliffs on Chesapeake Bay, where slender, ungainly trees with foot-long leaves grow to the water's edge. One day, we smelled a familiar fruit-salad odor but were unable to place it. Later, looking across the woods, we saw a deer eating a banana-colored cucumber from the ground. Pawpaws. We began to look on the ground, and sure enough, the greenish, yellow and brown fruits were everywhere.

Pawpaw trees (*Asimina triloba*) are quick-growing rangy plants rarely exceeding twenty feet but bearing outsized, broad, tapered leaves. Their small flowers are whitish green in May and bloom close to the leaf axis of the branches. The fruit usually falls to the ground before it is good to eat, but held at room temperature pawpaws will ripen. I like to eat one or two each season but there is little passionate love between us. I think I object to the slickity feeling of pawpaws rather than to the taste.

Pawpaws make a tasty banana bread. I have mashed the pulp from ripe pawpaws and substituted it for bananas in several recipes. With the substitution, we enjoy those recipes calling for one teaspoon of cinnamon and one-half cup of nuts better than plain pawpaw bread with no spice or nuts.

Though you can't smell elderberries before you pick them, for days after you have handled them your pores reek of elder. The black-berried elder (*Sambucus canadensis*), in addition to being used in jellies, preserves, wines, pies and as a cooked fruit, may be juiced, canned and prepared into a relish or chutney.

Cooking seems to dissipate the offensive eldery flavor. I use lemon with elderberries for pies, jellies and canned fruit. A friend of mine cans elder juice by boiling a bag of spices (cloves, nutmeg and cinnamon) with the slightly sweetened juice. She says her family loves it heated for winter breakfast before their two-mile trek to the school bus.

Although elderberries may be added to any kind of fruit and made into an intriguing wine, for a simple brew remove the larger stems from a gallon of black elderberries, add a gallon of water and boil for one-half hour. Cool to lukewarm and strain. Add enough boiled, but cooled, water to make six quarts. Stir in six cups of sugar, two thinly sliced lemons, a box of raisins and a package of yeast which has been dissolved in one cup of warm water. Work the wine for fourteen days in a covered crock or bucket, strain and siphon into sterilized bottles. Cork lightly and when the corks stay down, seal. Elderberry wine, like an agreeable friend, rises to any occasion and helps you out in time of need.

For elderberry pie, remove stems from a quart of berries without crushing them. Add three tablespoons of cornstarch, one-and-a-quarter cups of sugar, five tablespoons of lemon juice (or vinegar) and a dash of salt. Stir to coat the berries, then bake in a double-crusted pie at 400° F. for forty-five minutes, or until done. Elderberries cook into a hearty flavorful pie with no suggestion of their raw mustiness.

My grandmother used to dry ripe elderberries on screens in the August sun. No oven treatment was necessary, she said, because the rank raw fruit was too mean to be bothered by bugs. She made pies, fritters and a sweet, thick soup from the reconstituted dried fruit.

For fritters she simmered a cupful of dried elderberries in a pan of water until plump and then drained them through a sieve.

In a small iron skillet she melted one tablespoon of butter and stirred in three-fourths of a cup of flour mixed with two tablespoons of sugar, and when it was mashed into a lumpy dry mess, she poured in a half-cup of milk and put it over a low flame, stirring like crazy until it boiled into a smooth thick paste.

She then cooled the pale goo, added the grated rind of one lemon, one cup of drained elderberries, three beaten eggs, a pinch of soda and a dash of salt. She tried not to squash the elderberries too much.

Grandma heated a large frying pan half full of oil, and when it began to get restless she dropped in the elderberry batter from a teaspoon. After the fritters browned on each side, she removed them with a skimmer, drained them on paper and served them hot with a little powdered sugar.

Grandaddy and I used to eat a whole platterful of her puffy elderberry fritters, and though I preferred them plain, he used to dunk them in wine and smack his lips with each mouthful.

One wild food harvested in August which my family especially enjoys is young pods of milkweed (*Asclepias syriaca*). They compare it to fried okra. Crisp, mild-flavored, and somewhat slippery on the inside, milkweed pods fried in cornmeal/flour, half and half, are not unlike fried oysters.

The seedpods should be picked when they are very immature, about two inches long, before they become tough or elastic to the touch. The pods should be washed and dumped into boiling water, where they immediately turn vivid green. I throw off the first, second and third waters after a four-minute boiling in each, and that seems to extract the bitterness from the milky juice.

The three times boiled and drained pods are next poured onto a board and split lengthways. Each moist half is salted, dipped in cornmeal/flour dust, and fried until lightly browned and crusty. Everyone who has tasted fried milkweed pods commends their surprising good taste.

Some early August mornings, after a thundershower the evening before, I like to go alone to a draw near the garden and search for newborn puffballs (*Lycoperdon perlatum*). If I am lucky, I cut a pint or so. Back at the cabin, I dash the eggshell-white spheres under cold water to remove the tiny granular prickles that dot their golf-ball-like tops. While the coffee is perking, I slice them thin, then sauté them in butter in a lidded skillet. When they are limp and heated through, but not fried, I set them aside in a saucer and whip up a simple omelet seasoned with salt, pepper, a nibble of chives and a bit of nutmeg. I add part of the mushrooms to the beaten eggs and save the remainder to garnish the omelet a moment before it is served. Puffballs and country eggs start the day right.

The common puffball, which is about two inches wide and tall, grows throughout most of the temperate zone, usually in woods or pastures. They vary from tiny rounded balloons to white spheres with warts or prickles on their surface. Puffballs have no gills as such; their flesh is firm and white, and if eaten when very young they possess a delicate taste.

Although puffballs pop up any time of the year when the soil is warm, they seem to be most prevalent after a warm rain.

Larger species of puffballs may also be eaten when young and white, or nearly white, and are excellent sliced and fried like a slab of meat in a covered skillet so that they swim in their own rich juices.

I cook most puffballs in butter because their taste is elusive and easily overcome by stronger fats.

AUGUST

August is traditionally the month of tall drinks and easy living.

Betula lenta sounds like the name of a pretty girl. Sweet birch (*Betula lenta*) is the pretty girl of forests. The young buds, leaves and twigs of sweet birch contain a cousin (in taste) to oil of wintergreen and impart an aromatic flavoring to tea. Boiled for one minute, chilled and served with sugar and ice, *Betula lenta* is a light summer drink that children particularly like.

Sumac (*Rhus*) sounds as fearful as *Betula* sounds attractive, but sumac makes an equally refreshing, though acid, drink. Sumacade is similar to lemonade. The woody shrub with its velvety branches and feathery leaflets is familiar to all who have traveled past dry open fields from Maine to Manitoba and southward. *Rhus glabra*, or smooth sumac, grows on our Culpeper County place, and my husband gathers the fully ripe, red, tightly clustered berries before a thundershower. He puts the whole heads into the dishpan, covers them with cool spring water and beats them with a block of wood. He then borrows several of my tea towels and strains the juice two times to remove the malic acid hairs and any other debris. Sumacade is superb on a hot afternoon. It may be sweetened or drunk straight. Lewis experimented with sumac collins, which our collins-fancying friends enjoyed so thoroughly they got stuck in the mud sideways on our hill as they were driving home. To get them out we had to cut a new road, which has now grown back in sumac.

There is little danger of picking poison sumac by mistake because the poison berries are white and grow in loose, lacy clumps, while the edible *Rhus* are red and grow in tight clumps.

The mint family (*Labiatae*) known by their square stems, their smell and opposite leaves, may be brewed into savory tea or chilled and served as a pick-me-up on a sultry August day.

Sage, thyme and marjoram teas are tasty when boiled for a minute with a bouillon cube, chilled and sipped during the mid-afternoon doldrums.

The true mints peppermint and spearmint, as well as bergamot and horehound, add zip to a steamy summer morning. My grandmother used to steep tea by boiling two tablespoons of mint leaves with two tablespoons of diced lemon peel; she then cooled the brew and gave it to me to drink on a hot day. Often she floated a red bergamot flower in my drink, saying that the fragrant balm would draw out my sweetness and discourage the grumps. I always wanted sugar in my tea but she preferred her iced lemon-mint tea plain.

My grandfather made nettle tea from the young tops of the common stinging nettle (*Urtica*) which he drank on hot days. Although I do not know, I suspect Uncle Steve's nettle tea was alcoholic because many of his drinking friends praised it.

Nettles grow along roadsides throughout temperate North America and are easily recognized by their coarsely toothed leaves with their fine, stinging bristles.

To a gallon of young nettle tops Grandpa added two pinches of dry hop flowers and three bruised ginger roots, and he boiled them in a cloth bag in two gallons of water for thirty minutes. He turned off the fire and added two sliced lemons, a half-can of dark malt extract, and five pounds of sugar, stirring the mixture until the sugar dissolved. When the liquid was lukewarm, he poured it into a crock and added a cake of yeast which had been dissolved in a cup of water with a teaspoon of sugar, and he filled the crock with water to make five gallons of tea.

My grandfather let the nettle tea ferment for seven or eight days until he could no longer see it working, and then he strained it, bottled the remaining liquid and capped each bottle with a metal capper. He stored this tea for a few weeks before he chilled and served it.

A drink that we used to favor on a turbid August day was

root beer made from the fresh roots of sassafras (*Sassafras albidum*) combined with the dried roots of wild sarsaparilla (*Aralia nudicaulis*). My grandfather gathered sassafras roots after a thunderstorm, when they were easy to pull. After washing and grinding a quart of the roots, he covered them with water and boiled them with a cup of coarsely ground dried sarsaparilla root. He used a large flywheel coffee grinder to chop the tough roots. When the boiling liquid was strong and scarlet, he strained one cup of extract into a crock, added four pounds of sugar and enough tepid water to make five gallons of root beer. He dissolved one teaspoon of yeast (one-half yeast cake) in a cup of warm water and stirred it into the crock. Sometimes he colored the root beer with a browned sugar that he made by putting two tablespoons of sugar into a small tin cup, letting it melt and brown over a fire while he stirred constantly, and then adding two tablespoons of boiling water. When the sugar had dissolved and the liquid was rich brown, he added it to the crock.

The root beer was bottled immediately in sterilized jars and capped with metal caps. The bottles were then set on their sides in a warm spot under the kitchen sink for four days before he chilled them and let us drink the fizzy brew that tickled our noses.

Whether it is made from commercial extract or from scratch, curing root beer should be shut inside several boxes as a protection against flying glass; now and then a jar explodes.

Homemade root beer has a tendency to be psychotic and must be handled with tenderness. Neither alcoholic nor a bona fide member of the coffee-Coke circuit, root beer has manic phases and sometimes it is depressed. It may be hebephrenic, bubbly and giggly or it may lie in your glass in a catatonic trance.

Schizophrenic though it be, icy root beer creates a naturally refreshing pause during which you may contemplate the earth's goodness on a sultry August afternoon.

IX
Gathering
SEPTEMBER

September harvesting during the waning Virgo moon. First week under Libra. Harvesting potatoes, sweet potatoes and peanuts. Tomatoes: canning, cold and hot pack; catsup. Pickled watermelon rinds, cucumbers and peppers. Crab apples in pickles and jelly. Pickling wild foods: Indian cucumbers and artichokes. Herb gathering. Coffee substitutes: chicory, acorn, cleaver. Scuppernong wine, dried muscadine grapes. Plant winter-cress. Clam digging; razors fried and soft-shells steamed. September is a time to gather yourself for winter.

SEPTEMBER IS traditionally the time for harvesting and storing most garden vegetables. Moon-sign followers believe that harvesting should be done during the waning moon; those root crops that are to be used for seed should be dug during the third quarter, and other harvesting may be done during either the third or fourth quarter of the moon. They also point out that dry, barren zodiac signs are conducive to successful harvesting. Virgo (August 23 to September 23), astrologers say, is ideal for digging root crops because it is earthy as well as dry. If the third quarter of the moon coincides with Virgo's reign, beets, carrots, chicory, peanuts, potatoes and turnips may be dug with confidence. Believers say that root vegetables dug while the virgin Virgo extends his rich, cool influence will not only keep exceptionally well but will endow those who eat them with honesty, a virtue of Virgo.

The garden in Libra (September 23 to October 23) balances moist, semifruitful characteristics with airy, masculine tendencies. Thus, anything goes. If the moon is in the third or fourth quarter during the last week of September, harvesting may be done at that time.

Early potatoes can be left in the ground until September if they have been hilled properly to protect them from light and heat. They must be watched, however, for if summer temperatures have been high and rainfall heavy, potatoes should be harvested earlier. We usually dig potatoes as we need them, but the late crop and what is left from the first planting are dug in September. Potatoes should be harvested during the early morning hours and moved promptly from the garden to a shaded area to prevent sun and wind damage.

For winter holding, potatoes should cure about ten days at room temperature, because cuts will not heal properly if the tubers are placed immediately in cool storage. When cured, potatoes should be spread two to four deep in bins in a dark cellar or in pits. I cover the bins lightly with paper.

Ideally, potatoes should be dug in September, handled gently while being sorted and cured, and the best ones transferred to a dark, moderately moist, airy cellar. One year we didn't dig the last of our potatoes because a gigantic convention of yellow jackets met in our garden. After a freeze, when we were certain the yellow jackets were dead, we dug potatoes. They were sweet and rather watery, but edible. Frosted potatoes do not keep well, but if they are held at room temperature, for a week, the sweetness is eliminated, and if then put into cold storage they will not readily rot.

Sweet potatoes do not bear cold weather too well. They should be dug carefully in September, or as soon as the danger of frost is predicted. Because sweet potatoes bruise easily, they should be put directly into the small flat boxes or half-bushel baskets in which they will be stored.

Sweet potatoes need curing for a couple of weeks in moist heat, 80° or 90° F., and I usually bundle my boxes in blankets around the hot-water heater. Later I move the boxes under the crawl space, where the temperature is cool and even. The most important rule to remember regarding handling sweet potatoes is gentleness.

Peanuts are a fun crop. Like sweet spuds they are temperamental about the weather; when frost flags are up, dig them. Peanuts should be cured for two weeks at room temperature before brining or roasting them. The one time we produced any quantity of peanuts and beat the field mice to them in the ground, chipmunks stole them from the porch overnight. You can't trust wildlife.

Most gardens in September look tired, but like many tired-looking older people, the September garden still holds a lot of oomph. Tomato is the password.

Stewed, fried, juiced, puréed, pasted, preserved, cocktailed, catsupped, pickled, or sandwiched with bacon, the tomato is king of our garden. There is no wealth in the world like being tomato rich.

After eating and giving away all we are able, our family dives into canning. Tomatoes may be either hot packed or cold packed. If you are partial to neat tomatoes, cold, or raw, pack is your bag. If you merely want them put into cans, hot pack is simpler.

I usually use the hot-pack method, but if I have a batch of perfect medium-to-small globes, I pop them into jars whole for cold-packed tomatoes. A bushel of tomatoes will can into about twenty quarts. Using firm, ripe tomatoes, wash them and scald them for one minute. They may be submerged in boiling water by the colanderful, or boiling water may be poured over a dishpanful. As soon as the skins loosen, dip the fruit into cold water and drain. Cores and green areas are removed with the skins.

Each skinned fruit is dropped whole or quartered into hot, sterilized jars. When the tomatoes fill the jar to within one-half inch from the top, press them gently with a knife to fill the spaces with juice. A few more raw tomatoes are added, together with a teaspoon of salt, to each quart. The jar rims are wiped, the lids are adjusted, and the cold-packed tomato quarts are processed in a boiling water bath for an hour.

If you wish to hot-pack tomatoes, drop the skinned fruits into a large pan, boil them for five minutes, stirring so they will not burn. Pour the tomatoes into hot, sterilized jars, leave one-half inch head space, add one teaspoon of salt to each quart, wipe the rim and threads of the jar to remove seeds or pulp, which may hinder sealing, put on the jar tops and seal. Process quarts in a boiling-water bath for thirty minutes.

It is important to be sure that the canner water is nearly the same temperature as the jars. Hot jars put into cold water will break, and cold jars in hot water will lose their bottoms equally fast. A bottomless jar that is swimming around in icky, free-floating fruit in a canner is a mess.

Another warning: When you remove the hot jars from the canner do not set them on a cold surface. I did this once with tomatoes canned on the outdoor fireplace at the country. Looked great marching in a line along the rock after I had taken them from the canning kettle! But they didn't seal, and when I moved them to see why, nine neat glass bottoms stayed on the cold rock shelf and I had stewed tomatoes all over the place. Usually, however, canning tomatoes is one of the funnest chores in homemaking.

The smell of catsup simmering on the cookstove would make a warlock wed a witch, my grandfather would say as he stepped into the kitchen and inhaled to his toes. My husband eats tomato catsup on everything: eggs, bread—he even tried some on vanilla ice cream and pronounced it good.

For tangy tomato catsup: Chunk a peck of unpeeled but washed tomatoes with six medium but peeled onions and boil them together until soft. Rub them through a colander and then through a sieve. Return the pulp to the fire and add two tablespoons of salt, a cup of sugar, three bay leaves, a pinch of red pepper and a tablespoon each of powdered mace, black pepper and cloves. Add one tablespoon of celery seed which has been tied in a cloth bag. Boil the "new catsup" over a low fire, uncovered, for five or six hours, stirring it often. Remove the celery-seed bag and add a pint of vinegar. Bring the catsup to a boil again and simmer for five minutes, stirring constantly. Remove it from the fire, bottle and seal.

To add contrasting color to tomato time, my grandmother picked a peck of green tomatoes for pickle relish. She sliced them very thin and layered them in a crock with a cup of salt sprinkled equally between each layer. The following day she rinsed them in cold water, drained them in a colander, added twenty sliced onions, two pounds of dark-brown sugar, six tablespoons of whole pickling spice and about two quarts of vinegar. She simmered these ingredients for about three-fourths of an hour, stirring often, and poured the boiling, thick relish into hot, sterilized jars for sealing.

Labor Day was celebrated with an enormous neighborhood picnic when I was a teen-ager. Our family fried a bushel of chicken. Other households would bring a dishpanful of potato salad or a half-dozen pies. Uncle Steve rolled out a couple of kegs and Uncle Otto arrived with a wagonful of watermelons.

Later in the evening when the melons were cut and seed-spitting contests were completed, Grandma would inspect the leftover slices and select the thickest rinds.

The next day she pickled watermelon rind. She dissolved six cups of brown sugar in a quart of vinegar and into a spice sack she crumbled four ounces of cinnamon and two ounces of cloves. She boiled the spices and sweetened vinegar for ten minutes and poured it over about two quarts of pared and sliced watermelon rind. She let the pickle stand for twenty-four hours, then drained off the spiced vinegar, reheated it to a boil and poured it over the rind again. She let the pickle stand for a second twenty-four hours. Then she boiled the pickle and rind together for ten minutes and packed them into hot, sterilized jars, covered them with the boiling liquid and sealed them. Each time we nibbled a rind thereafter we remembered the heaps of fun and food of September.

Grandma would pickle anything at the hint of a new idea. Cucumbers, of course, were her standbys, and sweet cucumber pickles were and are my favorite.

Soak forty or fifty small, washed and dried cucumbers for three days in a brine that floats an egg. Drain them and lay them in cold, fresh water for a day. Line an enamel pan with grape leaves and layer cucumbers with a sprinkle of alum between each layer in the pan. Cover with cold water and four or five layers of grape leaves. Cover pan with lid and steam the cucumbers over a very low fire for six hours. Drain cucumbers and toss into cold water. Drain them immediately, pack into hot, sterilized jars, and fill the jars with boiling vinegar which has been cooked with sugar and spices for ten minutes. (To make the pickle liquid, for each cup of vinegar add one cup of sugar and a tablespoon each of cloves, crushed cinnamon, allspice, peppercorns, mace, tarragon and chervil.) Seal the jars at once and store in a cool place.

For dills, Grandma washed and dried forty or fifty small cucumbers and put them in a pickle made of six cups of vinegar, six cups of water, one-and-one-half cups of sugar, three-quarters of a cup of salt and six tablespoons of mixed pickling spices. She simmered them in a large enamel pan for thirty minutes. She put a head of dill into each hot, sterilized half-gallon jar and packed the jar with hot cucumbers. On the top of each jar she placed a second head of dill and one small clove of garlic. She reheated the vinegar pickle to boiling and filled each jar, then lidded and sealed the pickles for processing. Grandma boiled her half-gallons of dill pickles thirty minutes in a boiling-water bath and did not allow them to be eaten until Thanksgiving.

To my family's way of thinking pickled pepper rings rank as tops. Wash, drain and slice enough green and red sweet (Bell) peppers to make one gallon of pepper circles sliced one-quarter-inch thick. (The tops and centers are removed from the peppers before slicing.) Dissolve one-and-one-half cups of salt in one gallon of water and pour over the peppers. Let them stand overnight. Rinse in cold water and drain. Pack the pepper rings gently into hot, sterilized jars; shake down to pack them tightly. Heat to a rolling boil a pickling liquid made of four cups of white vinegar, one-and-one-half cups of sugar, eight whole cloves, eight or ten peppercorns, six allspice and six blades of mace. Fill the pepper-packed jars with the boiling spiced vinegar and seal at once. Pickled peppers should be fit to eat in three months.

In September I give any kid who is willing five cents a quart to pick up fallen crab apples. Pickled crab apples go well in school lunches. I select one gallon of wormless red crab apples with stems, and after washing and sorting, I poke each apple with a darning needle so it will not explode when cooking.

In a large pot I put five cups of sugar in four cups of vinegar, add two tablespoons of ground cinnamon, one tablespoon of allspice and one-half tablespoon of cloves which have been tied in a cloth, and boil the mixture until the sugar dissolves. When it cools to lukewarm I add the pricked apples. Then I simmer it very gently until the crab apples are soft, and I let the whole thing stand overnight in a cool place. The next day I heat the pot of vinegar and apples to boiling, pack the hot crab apples into hot, sterilized pint jars, reheat the syrup to boiling again and pour it over the apples. Each jar is sealed tightly and stored until Thanksgiving.

Ornamental flowering crab-apple jelly has been my singular original contribution to local suburban living. Our place is blessed with three old mother trees that never fail to bring forth fruit. (Except the year the State Highway Department spread fertilizer in a windstorm and clouds of lime covered the neighborhood. I looked out the window and thought our pink-blooming trees had disappeared. The fertilizer was too much for the local bees, too, because not one crab apple developed.)

After washing and sorting, I load a heavy pot with the small apples and cover them with water. The fruit is boiled twenty minutes or until the juice is deeply colored. After it is cooled, I put the fruit and juice through a heavy, unbleached jelly sack. The clue to quick crab-apple jelly is squeezing or twisting the bag until sticky jelly oozes through the cloth and no more liquid can be manually pressed from the apples.

Using the standard proportions—four cups of juice to three cups of sugar—I boil the stock into a ruby jelly. While it is boiling, I wash and sterilize jars. When the liquid has boiled up and starts to retreat, or to boil down from its high mark on

the side of the pan, I watch it and start testing for the jellying point. This takes about twenty minutes from the time it
starts to boil. When the jellying point is reached, the last
drops of jelly will run together and flake off the spoon. I then
pour the hot jelly into hot, sterilized jars and either vacuum-
seal them at once or cover the jelly with paraffin when it is
almost cold. Crab-apple jelly costs very little to make, it has
a sharp taste, and it makes into a naturally pretty red spread.

Wild foods also may be preserved into sweet- and sour-
pickle happiness.

Indian cucumbers (*Medeola virginiana*) may be eaten
raw, cubed in salad or pickled. They grow in sociable groups
and, like other sociables, are best when mildly pickled. The
plants, upright and somewhat woody, remind me of dogwood
seedlings. The single slender stems of Indian cucumbers grow
out of a whorl of five or seven dark, elongate, visibly ribbed
leaves. There is often a second circle of three or four leaves
near the top of the plant from which a few spindly cream-
colored flowers bloom and are followed by small black berries. The roots grow horizontally just below the ground surface, making the cucumbers easy to dig. Indian cucumbers
are found from the Great Lakes eastward and south to Florida
in rich woodlands.

Although they may be dug in the spring, Indian cucumbers are easier to identify during the late summer or early
fall because their leaves then turn a maroon color. Spring or
fall, they are crispy, cool and mildly cucumberish in flavor.

My grandmother used to make an herb vinegar for Indian
cucumbers by crushing washed fresh young leaves of tarragon, chervil or savory into a jar filled with vinegar. She
corked it and shook it daily for about a week. To make Indian-
cucumber pickles, she would strain the vinegar over the cucumbers which had been washed, chunked, soaked for an
hour in a mild brine and rinsed. After tossing them in the
vinegar, she added olive oil, pepper and salt. Though remi-

niscent of garden cucumbers, the wild root has its own texture and distinctive flavor.

I have made good artichoke pickles by digging a gallon of Jerusalem artichokes (*Helianthus tuberosa*) the last of September or immediately after they bloom, when their skins have not browned and the earth creatures have not eaten chunks out of them. I wash and drain the knobby roots and immerse them in a mild brine (one-half cup of salt to a gallon of water) overnight, then rinse them with clear, cold water and drain.

In one-half gallon of vinegar, I boil two cups of sugar, two tablespoons of mixed pickling spices, one clove of garlic, six peppercorns and one tablespoon of turmeric. The spices are tied in a bag and the spiced liquid is boiled about twenty minutes. I pack the brined and rinsed artichokes into hot, sterilized pint jars, cover them with the boiling pickle syrup and seal them.

These pickles have never lasted long enough for me to know whether they get soft. We usually eat them in about six weeks and they are sweet-sour and satisfying.

Culinary herbs may be grown and dried with unbelievable ease. My grandmother had an herb garden of which she was quite protective and proud. When she found a neighbor's cat frisking in her fennel, I thought she was going to climb the fence right after it. That was a bad day. She found worms in her anise and the hens reached through the wire and pecked her parsley. Parsley and fennel are slow-starting herbs and need to be babied.

For full flavor, herbs should be gathered when their oils are at their highest. Harvesting herbs is not related to a generalized time of year. Most leaf herbs and flowering heads are gathered throughout the summer. Seeds are harvested before they shatter and turn dull. Roots may be dug in the early fall, when they are full. Perennial herb plants may be cut back to about two-thirds of their mature height, and herbs to be brought indoors for the winter, such as chives, may be potted when frost is knocking at the door.

Culinary herbs to be dried should be rinsed, shaken free of excess moisture and, when processed, stored in labeled containers.

My grandmother used to dry culinary herbs in bundles or spread them on screens in the sun. Today plant analysts suggest gathering herbs in the morning after the dew has evaporated and spreading them on papers or gauze in a warm dry room for four or five days to dry. Herb roots should be washed, sliced thin, and spread to dry in a warm room. Seeds are simply dried for a few days on a shelf. When perfectly dry, herbs should be put into opaque or dark containers with a tight lid, labeled and kept in a handy location.

Someone once said that excessive use of herbs, like an overpowering woman, drives away admirers. Herb flavors should be secretively suggestive; used properly, they engage in a love affair with the taste buds. It must be remembered, however, that some taste buds tend to be fickle and to fall in love with new flavors every few days. Some tasters play the field and court two flavors at the same time. Other tongue sensors are faithful lovers of the same herbs.

Culinary herbs to be used in cold foods should be presoaked and added several hours before serving. Heat releases herbal flavors and may be added to hot foods ten to thirty minutes before a meal.

Grandmother's garden consisted of:

Basil (*Ocymum minimum*). Leaves gathered when the plants are starting to bloom are dried and may be used in soups, vegetables, meats and eggs. Fresh basil is superior, but it holds only a short time.

Borage (*Borago officinalis*). Leaves gathered when plants are mature may be used in pickles and in salads. Fresh borage leaves are best, but leaves and flowers may be dried for winter use.

Burnet salad (*Poterium sanguisorba*). Young leaves may be used in wine flavoring when dried on the stalk. Fresh burnet leaves add a hint of cucumber to salads.

CARAWAY (*Carum carvi*). Seeds may be used in baking and in liqueurs. The plants should be cut well above the roots as soon as the seeds ripen because the seeds fall very quickly. The whole plant should be dried on paper.

CHERVIL (*Anthriscus cerefolium*). Leaves harvested in the young leafy stage may be used fresh in salads and sauces. Dried, the leaves ,are good in soups where they impart an anise-caraway flavor that is pleasant to taste.

CUMIN (*Cuminum cyminum*). Dried seeds may be used in curry and North African dishes, in pickles, chili con carne and lamb. The plant heads are cut when mature and laid on paper to dry.

DILL (*Anethum graveolens*). Seeds may be used in sauces, bread and pickles. When the plant turns reddish it should be cut and laid on paper to dry because dill seeds drop quickly when dried. Fresh dill leaves may be chopped finely for salads, and my grandmother used the seed heads with the fresh leaves in pickles.

ELECAMPANE (*Inula helenium*). The rounded, horny roots are dug in the fall and are used in cakes and candy. Young roots may be sliced and dried, and fresh root may be candied.

HORSE-RADISH (*Armoracia rorippa*). Roots may be dug at any time of year, grated and mixed with vinegar for use as a relish. Roots may be dried whole, grated and soaked in vinegar for a less bitey dressing.

LOVAGE (*Levisticum officinale* or *Ligusticum scoticum*). Leaves and young stems may be used fresh or dried in soups and sauces. Al-thought somewhat sweet, its taste is similar to celery. Its brownish seeds are spicy and are used in confections and cake flavoring.

MARJORAM (*Origanum onites*). Leaves gathered when young may be diced fresh into meat dishes or the plants cut when mature and hung to dry.

ROSEMARY (*Rosmarinus officinalis*). Leaves and flowers clipped when at full stage of bloom may be used in soups and salads, both fresh and as a dried herb. Meats are often improved by basting them with a rosemary twig which has been dipped in olive oil.

SAGE (*Salvia officinalis*). Young leaves may be used in stuffings, sausage and vegetables when dried. Fresh sage leaves may be brewed into a musty tea.

SAVORY (*Satureia montana*). Leaves picked when mature may be used fresh in eggs, cheese dishes and in tomatoes. As soon as the flowers appear, stalks should be cut for drying and use in sausage.

TARRAGON (*Artemisia dracunculus*). Leaves may be picked when the plant is just starting to bloom and may be used as a dried herb in vinegar, mustard and sauces.

THYME (*Thymus vulgaris*). Full blooms and leaves are cut and may
    be used fresh or dried for use in meats, salads and soups. This is
    one of the few herbs which will retain its flavor after a year.
WOODRUFF (*Asperula odorata*). Mature leaves and flowers may be
    used in beverages when dried or semidried on the stalk.

In addition to culinary herbs, colonial gardeners often
cultivated coffee substitutes which in later years escaped cultivation and now grow wild. Some people relish the taste of
coffee substitutes. Like any food or beverage, the product
should be weighed on its own merits. To taste parched and
perked seeds, roots or nuts with the thought "coffee" in mind
is unfair to the substitute.

Roasted chicory roots (*Cichorium intybus*) do not taste like
coffee, but when used as an additive, some people believe,
they improve the color and flavor of South American coffee.

Chicory leaves resemble dandelions when young, but as
the plants mature, a rigid, loosely branched two-foot stem develops, and blue flowers bloom in midsummer. Chicory grows
on roadsides and in waste clay soils from Canada southward.
The tubular roots, which grow horizontally in the ground,
should be dug in September after flowering is over.

To be used as a coffee additive, the roots should be washed,
coarse-ground, dried in a very slow oven for two or three
hours, then roasted in a clean skillet. The roasting or browning process should be done very slowly and the granulated
chicory should be repeatedly stirred until the proper color
and flavor are reached. The chicory may then be ground a second time and dry-roasted again if the flavor and color do not
quite meet your taste. Roasting is a personal matter and
should be done a little at a time until the desired taste is
achieved.

The roasting (or dry-frying, as you would brown flour) is
often done in a frying pan and is the most important factor
in good chicory-blended coffee. We dig roots, select only the
brittle ones, wash, chop, dry and roast them, then grind and

roast again before mixing them half and half with medium-priced commercial coffee.

Chicory coffee should be perked slowly for from four to eight minutes. To cook it longer encourages a rank taste. Once brewed, it should not be allowed to boil a second time. If you are like me and reheat and drink coffee all day until the pot is dry, do not let the reheated chicory coffee boil or you will regret it. You will also regret losing your breakfast. Twice-boiled chicory is sickening.

I have heard of roasting dried persimmon seeds (*Diospyros*), wild senna seeds (*Cassia occidentalis*), and sunflower seeds (*Helianthus*) and crushing them into "coffee." Dandelion root (*Taraxacum*) has been ground, roasted and used as a coffee substitute, but my only experiment with the dandelion brew left me shriveled. Dandelion coffee tasted as bitter as wormwood, or, as my grandmother would say, "like the tops of an old woman's shoes."

My ancient neighbor with the topaz cheeks—the one who told me about acorn bread—also said that during hard times her family roasted acorns as a coffee substitute. Using black or red-oak acorns, they boiled the whole, dry nuts for half a day in a kettle containing one-third hardwood ashes and two-thirds water. The acorns were drained, rinsed and boiled a second and third time in clear water, then dried, the shells removed, and the kernels roasted. The result was a small brown bean, not unlike a coffee bean, she said. Acorn beans were ground and used as coffee.

Acorn coffee may be perked plain, but my friend preferred to fry the roasted and ground nuts in a heavy skillet with about a tablespoon of fat. This second roasting, she admitted, was "lucky." She believed in eating one fried dish each meal for luck.

Cleaver, or goose grass (*Galium aparine*), a mad member of the madder family, is a versatile plant; no wonder it suffers insecurity and clings compulsively to all who pass by.

Cleavers have been used as a potherb; a medicinal herb to encourage the "longe, leane, lanke looke"; a chicken feed; a strainer to clean hairs and straw from milk; and the seeds are roasted into an agreeable coffee substitute.

Cleavers grow in Alaska, southward across Canada and into Texas, and are found on seashores and in rocky woods. Although cleaver sprouts may be eaten in the spring, the tiny twin burr seeds ripen later.

The weak, elongate cleaver plants have crooked, scratchy stems; the slender leaves grow in whorls of seven or eight, and inconspicuous white flowers cluster in the leaf axils. *Galium aparine* seeds are gathered by spreading sheets at the bases of the sprawling plants when the burrs brown. They are dried, the seeds are shaken free of the burrs and roasted lightly on cookie tins in a slow oven for twenty to thirty minutes. These seeds are less than one-eighth of an inch in diameter and are usually not ground. After roasting, they are simply brewed into coffee. Actually, the taste and smell of cleaver is similar to full-bodied coffee. I have found cleaver brew to be pleasant and mildly stimulating; the hardship of utilizing this wild food is the difficulty of gathering the tiny seeds.

September is scuppernong time. A Georgia gentlewoman, quiet-spoken, noble in her mild manners, once brought me a sack of grapes from "home." I had never seen the big, sweet, aromatic fruit and to me it somehow embodied the South.

After setting aside a few grapes for drying, I made a mini-batch of scuppernong amber. One of the beauties of making your own wine is that you can savor both the fruit and the memories long after the ripe fruit is gone. The golden clarity of the Georgia wine is like a sunset. Its quiet beauty reminds me of my neighbor.

For a taste of scuppernong in the bottle, I picked the unwashed grapes from the stems, and in an enamel kettle mashed two quarts of them with one pound of white sugar.

After the sugar was dissolved, I put the grapes in the basement overnight. The following day I added one quart of
boiling water and covered the pot, allowing it to ferment for
three weeks. I stirred the grapes, and when no further fermenting was noticeable, I strained them through a sack,
settled the juice for one day, and poured it carefully into two
bottles. The wine is still sealed, but just before I bunged the
corks home I kept out a taste for my husband and me.

The scuppernongs I dried were processed with some tough
but tasty muscadines (*Vitis rotundifolia*) according to the
remarkable Dr. Carver's recipe.* I covered the ripe, washed
grapes with boiling water and simmered them in an enamel
kettle until they were hot through, reddish in color, but still
unbroken. Next, I stirred in a scant tablespoonful of baking
soda to a gallon of stemmed fruit and mixed them gently for
three minutes. I poured off the soda water and washed the
grapes three more times in cold water. I then drained them
and dried them in a low oven for thirty minutes, then stored
the grapes in sterilized, lidded jars.

Dried grapes may be eaten as raisins with seeds, or reconstituted by simmering thirty minutes in water, seeded, and
used as fresh grape pulp in cooking or jam. I have dried different varieties of grapes. The scuppernongs lost flavor and
color, the fox grapes and the small wild grapes became sour;
the muscadines seemed to retain sweetness and flavor the best.

In addition to gathering September grapes for wine, jellies,
marmalades, preserves and juices, there is one last autumn
chore to accomplish before freeze-up; that is to sow cress
(*Barbarea vulgaris* and *verna*). Although plain cress may be
sowed all the year round, some people sow it as a ground
cover and winter green after most vegetables have been
harvested. Traditionally, cress is planted during the first
quarter of the moon in Libra for continued winter greens.
Freezing does not seem to harm cress, but if it lies under the

* George Washington Carver, *Nature's Garden for Victory and Peace* (revised),
Tuskegee Institute, Bulletin 43, Tuskegee, Alabama, 1942.

snow too long, it becomes wan. "Crease salad" is a favorite potherb of many country people, who season it with fatback. I boil cress in two waters and serve it with diced crisp-fried bacon and drippings, or sometimes sprinkle each serving with vinegar.

The first week of wet Libra's reign, September 23 to 30, has long been recognized as clam-digging time. Most bivalves are fat and frisky in the fall. Clams are the sea's gift to foragers. Keeping tabs on tides, weather, and spots for good digging adds another dimension to a natural year. With little effort, clam digging provides food, fun and a chance to breathe unspoiled salty-sweet ocean air.

Anyone who has dug West Coast razor clams (*Siliqua patula*) knows that there is as much catching as digging to the operation. Razor clams move faster than most diggers. They can move any degree of the compass; they are sly with their siphons and sneaky with their feet. Razor clams sit up on end in the sand and are ready to depart at an instant's notice. The beach on Cook Inlet, Alaska, where I dug razors is level, deep-sanded and subject to full ocean waves. The clams themselves are hooked on juice, they abhor the dry life and are found at the low-tide line. Various species of razor clams frequent the low-tide flats of sandy beaches along both the Atlantic and Pacific coasts, and most are found at the low-tide line.

Razor clams' shells are brittle, whitish, with gray or brown stains, and their distinguishing characteristic, in addition to speed, is their oblong shape. *Siliqua patula*, West Coast razors, are five inches long, two inches wide, slim, rounded, with blunt ends. Though their necks or siphons are short, they are extremely muscular and capable of propelling the clam faster than a tadpole can squiggle. Razor clams can actually disappear into the sand before your eyes, but, like deer, when disturbed they retreat a short distance, then stop and listen.

With a little practice, it is possible to psych out razor clams.

Find a place where they are known to live, stand in the middle of the area, and stare at the wet sand. Soon little depressions will cave in, indicating spots that clams are preparing to vacate. The diggers, each armed with a spade, work in pairs. They appear to be engaged in a minuet. Facing each other along the tide line, they pause, then simultaneously thrust their spades down into the sand on either side of the depression, stoop, stand, and repeat the dance. The thrusts must be swift and the two spades must be close enough together to partly encircle the fleeing clam. There is only one chance to capture a razor clam; if it is flubbed, say goodbye to *that* elusive chowder maker and move on to another depression.

Siliqua patula seem to like communal living. I have never found a solitary razor clam. They live in groups just at low water and are said to stick their necks out during Libra and again during Pisces.

Because of their size, Alaskan razor clams are rarely fried whole or eaten raw. Most people steam them, grind them coarsely and make chowder, scallops, sausages, cutlets, tartlets, pies, Newburg or dumplings. Some clam eaters prefer to remove the meat from the shells before cooking by inserting a thin knife and severing the hinge muscles to open the shells. The shelled clams are cut into edible-size strips and fried, grilled, curried, fricasseed, battered, deviled or sherried.

My husband likes fried razor strips, corn sticks, and beach toddy for a late supper.

I give Lewis a toddy made of a jigger of bourbon, a dash of water and a pinch of nutmeg; then I roll each clam strip in fine cracker crumbs seasoned with salt and pepper. I let them stand for half an hour and then roll them in cornmeal. I fry the clams brown in olive or salad oil and they twist and curl like crisp confetti.

While the clams are standing, I beat two eggs very lightly, add one-half cup of flour, a cup and a half of cornmeal, one tablespoon of sugar, four teaspoons of baking powder, one teaspoon of salt, and at the last moment I mix in one cup of milk and three tablespoons of melted butter. I grease the heated iron corn-stick mold, fill each mold with batter and bake in a preheated oven at 450° F. for twenty minutes.

Clam strips and corn sticks in September furnish an interesting change of pace.

Another merry mollusk, abundant in both eastern and western temperate coastal waters, is the soft-shell clam (*Mya arenaria*). Around Chesapeake Bay, soft-shell clams are found primarily in offshore shallows and are taken by dredges, so seashore foraging is limited. Northward into Maine, however, all that is needed after law requirements are satisfied is a good back, a beach, a bucket and a spade. To let the soft-shells purge themselves of sand, some clam eaters put them in a washtub of water and float bread crumbs or cornmeal on top. However, those we buy at Broome's Island, Maryland, require no grit removal.

To steam soft-shell clams, Lewis heats a quart of beer in the canner with a rack, and when the beer is boiling, he dumps a bucket of washed clams into the pot. In fifteen minutes they are all open-jawed and ready for the table.

Each diner is served a cup of the beer-base clam broth and a small bowl of melted butter.

A friend at Broome's Island showed us how to take the cooked meat from the shell. Insert the thumbnail under the hinge muscle and lift out the clam. Holding the clam in the right hand, peel off the heavy skin of the neck and discard it. Then, using both thumbs, turn the opening of the siphon, or neck, inside out. To do this properly, slip the end of the neck over the tip of the right forefinger. The whole clam, particularly the inside-out neck which is still over the forefinger, is then washed up and down in the clam-nectar cup, dipped in the melted butter and popped into the mouth.

Nothing else is necessary when you have steamed soft-shell (or long-neck) clams by the bucketful and beer by the quart. When you cannot swallow one more tidbit of happiness, carefully sip the clam nectar from your cup, making sure to leave at the bottom the grit washed from the necks. Then sit back and groan with pleasure.

Seashore, garden or kitchen, September is a pleasureful month. It is a time to breath deeply and to gather yourself for winter.

X

Autumn Acts and Apple Butter
OCTOBER

Libra harvesting. Sweet and hard cider. Apple butter. Setting by the garden. The digging and care of roots; pumpkins and squash preserved, pumpkin wine. Corn-cob jelly. Tomato storage, green-tomato mincemeat. Daylily tubers, wild potatoes. Wild-herb gathering and care. Nuts: pickled nuts, gathering and removing nutmeats and oils the Indian way. Candy: horehound, spearmint, taffy, ginger crystallized. Cranberry wine. Persimmons in pudding and wine. Hunter's moon. With the hunt in October, a natural pulse is renewed.

Libra, an apple farmer once told me, is the time for "cutting." This does not mean cutting to destroy, he explained; rather, cutting is to encourage a stronger life to grow. Though Libra contains masculine characteristics, it is also an airy, moist and semifruitful sign.

Any crops harvested under Libra (September 23 to October 23), the farmer said, should be reaped during the old phase of the moon, the waning third or fourth quarter. This will counteract the moist influences of the Scales and any bruised spots will dry up. When fruit is picked during the new moon, the bruises will rot, he contended.

That farmer would not pick apples for cider or winter keeping until the sign of Libra; he believed that apples picked at that time would pass on a richer, fuller goodness to those who ate them. Elaborating, he said that apple trees should be planted during the watery sign of Pisces and the fruit harvested during the sign of Libra. "Water completes the cycle of life," he declared. His apples were superior—firm-ripe, aromatic, fine in color and shape.

My grandfather tried to wait until the waning moon under Scorpio (October 23 to November 22) to harvest apples. He raised winesaps for "keeping" and believed that Scorpio's watery and fruitful sign "fixed the sugar and juice" in his winter apples.

Late apples should be stored at about 31° F. My grandfather packed his storage apples between layers of straw in tight-lidded barrels; but I find that shallow boxes fitted with plastic laundry-cleaner bags preserve humidity and keep apples firm until spring. I poke holes in the polyethylene for

179

ventilation and store apples in a darkened mouseproof corner
of the cellar.

Even today, the smell of apples in the basement rings the
cider-time chimes of my memories.

Because my grandfather believed that different varieties of
apples made cider more interesting, he blended one part
delicious, or some other sweet apple, with one part winesap,
and a handful of crab apples for tartness.

It was my job to wash the cider fruit before the press
stopped by. In our neighborhood, a traveling apple press
driven by a rotund, apple-cheeked German served cider cus-
tomers each October. He had two rigs drawn by magnificent
Belgians and flanked by a donkey that turned the press wheel.
One wagon was built like a giant clothes wringer with
wooden cylinders that could devour a bushel of apples in one
gulp. The other wagon was a low-slung wooden tank into
which the apple juice flowed. The press operator traveled
from house to house pressing apples on shares—that is, for
every gallon of juice expressed he kept one-half gallon for
himself. He also kept the pulp, which he fed to stock. In spite
of his pink babyish look, the presser was opinionated and
stubborn. I remember someone asking him why he did not
buy a truck and tank. The round German swelled and ha-
rangued upon the evils of "unnatural power." His apple press
always drew a crowd, and he stood like an elfin tyrant shouting to his audience. His face grew red as he shouted that the
generalized use of petroleum and coal would destroy the
earth. "The gases of those machines are killing my horses!"
he yelled, trembling with the frustration of one who knows
that he is already defeated. He believed that to burn petroleum destroyed a part of the earth, that coal and oil could
not replace themselves. "They give only poisons back to the
world," he repeated.

The presser's hatred for "unnatural power" may have been
a premonition. He was hit by a truck and killed.

To make either sweet or hard cider, the juice pressed from

the apples should be strained through several thicknesses of cloth and allowed to settle. Sedimentation takes from one to three days, and the temperature should be held at 40° F. or below to retard fermentation. Cider may be drunk at any time after pressing.

If sweet cider is to be kept for longer than a week, it should be refrigerated at a temperature of between 32° and 36° F. It may be frozen in unbreakable containers filled 90 percent full, or it may be pasteurized by heating to 170° F. and held at that temperature for ten minutes.

To many people cider means a winelike low-alcoholic drink called hard cider. To obtain a mildly alcoholic cider my grandfather used to add about one-half pound of sugar to a gallon of sweet cider after it had settled. He mixed the sugar with a little water, heated it until dissolved, and added the clear sugar water to the cider barrel. He said that apple juice to be made into hard cider should not be heated because the pectin will become active and cause cloudiness.

When the sugar and juice are mixed, modern methods of cider making incorporate the addition of sodium metabisulphite at this time, to discourage bad yeast from growing.

My grandfather did not use anti-bad-yeast aids. After he mixed in the sugar-water solution, he added a package of yeast (dissolved in a cup of warm water and activated with a teaspoonful of sugar) to the apple juice and allowed it to ferment in a warm place for ten days to two weeks. He then siphoned the cider into sterilized gallon jars, being careful not to stir the sediment from the bottom of the barrel, and he attached a simple air lock to each gallon jug. My grandfather's fermentation locks consisted of a tight-fitting cork into which a hole had been drilled. A tube was forced into the cork hole to catch all escaping gases and the other end of the tube was put into a jar of water. The escaping gas from the cider went *blop, blop*, and when it stopped, Grandaddy removed the lock and sealed the jar.

Cider on highway fruit stands each October prods my husband's desire for apple butter. Burned apple butter was an annual feat at our house until my blessed neighbor sent me a recipe for apple butter in the oven.

Turn ten pounds of apples into unsweetened sauce and pour into an enamel roasting pan. Stir in approximately one-and-a-half quarts of cider, one tablespoon each of cinnamon, cloves and nutmeg, and five pounds of sugar. Cover the roaster, put the apple mixture into a 350° F. oven and stir occasionally until it boils. When boiling, turn the heat back to 250° F. and bake for five hours or until the butter is stiff. My neighbor said she sometimes turned the heat down to 200° F. after the sauce had boiled and left the apple butter in the low, low oven to roast all night. In the morning she ladled her thick apple butter into sterilized jars and sealed them. This easy recipe cooks into rich brown butter without plopping all over the stove and without burning.

Apple butter plopping in a thirty-five gallon copper kettle with pennies in the bottom is something else. Each plop wafts the scent of sweet apples into the crisp autumn sunshine. Neighbors smell it miles away and gather to "take their turn on the stick," and to visit around the fragrant fire.

About nine o'clock one Halloween morning, we arrived at the apple-butter making in a frosty clearing alive with scurrying farm folk, excited dogs and lively kids. The young men were splitting wood, the women were peeling apples and exchanging news, the girls were carrying water and trying to ignore the boys, and the children carried wood to a pile near the steaming blackened kettle.

Older men lounged near the parked cars and took their turns stirring the apple butter with a fourteen-foot paddle-ended pole. The thirty-inch paddle was attached at right angles to the pole, and two people were needed to move the paddle around in the boiling apples.

When we arrived, my husband was instructed to throw his pennies into the apple-butter pot. "If we get enough of them in the bottom, they move around and keep the butter from sticking," our country host advised. "Also, it's a dandy way to polish pennies," he added with a twinkle.

As soon as the hellos were exchanged, Lewis and I, being eager types, grabbed the stirring stick. Moving peeled, cored and quartered apples back and forth was heavy work. The fire blazed up when someone poked it or added wood, and we were warned to keep the apples moving so that they would not burn. Just as soon as the apples became mushy and easy to stir, someone would peer through the steam and pour in another bushel of apples. Then the muscle work of moving the apples started all over again. All day long the butter boiled, different teams stirred, more apples were added, the kids romped, and the men made frequent trips into the bushes for a nip.

By late afternoon several guitars and mandolins appeared. The men and women circled their chairs around the kettle and, timidly at first, everyone began to sing. They sang mountain songs, heart-tugging laments about the Government tearing their kin from their mountain homelands to make "The Park"; they sang rousing hoedown numbers, spirituals that made your spine shimmy, and tender love songs.

Long mountain shadows had crept up the valley when a newcomer arrived. Not until the obese older woman was assisted to a chair in the firelit circle did I sense that she was special, a grande dame of the mountains. After surveying the scene and nodding to relatives and friends, she tasted the butter and advised more fire under the kettle. Immediately a couple of young people brought more wood.

About nine o'clock at night, when a huge orange moon balanced on the treetops, and twenty-six bushels of apples had been boiled into a thick, plopping brown sauce, the heavyset grande dame asked for a spoon. In a flurry, a saucer of the butter was brought to her.

"Ready," she proclaimed, nodding her head in approval as if she alone had been responsible for the peeling and the tugging on the stick all day. The men were called in from the bushes, sugar and spices were lined up on a stump beside the apple-butter queen, and with great ceremony the butter was finished off. Sugar was added by the five-pound bag until the queen raised her hand, and then she herself stood to add the cloves, cinnamon, allspice and nutmeg.

The last half-hour of boiling, we were informed, was the most crucial. Sugar burns, I was told. Aware of my talents along those lines, I earnestly searched for someone to relieve me on the pole. Most of the men were too happy to care, and as for the others, I feared that they might end up in the apple butter, so I hung on with my partner, a strange hunter who had wandered in out of the woods. We stirred like hell.

Sitting like a true matriarch, the old woman watched like a hawk and pointed to places we missed as we stirred. Finally she announced that the apple butter was ready to bottle.

On a table a distance from the kettle and under the solitary string of lights stood sixty sterilized half-gallon jars ready for filling. The canning process had been rehearsed during the day and every bottling lady was at her post. Bottling was swift and efficient. Needless to say, the apple butter was superb.

We were in our car, ready to leave, when the first penny was found and one of the kids raced to show us. Held aloft, the copper coin reflected the moonlight from its brilliant surface as if the penny itself contained brightness and life. We still have our apple-butter penny, and although it is dull now, I am saving it with a handful of others for next October and a new go at the apple-butter kettle.

Garden chores for October generally consist of setting by, or tending to vegetables for the final time. Root crops such as beets, carrots and turnips not yet dug may be left in the ground until the nights reach freezing: 32° F. If you wish to dig them, however, root crops store best if their tops are cut about one-half inch above their crown. Some gardeners wash and dry their root vegetables before storing, but if the soil is dry when they are dug, washing is not necessary. As with potatoes, excessive exposure to wind and sun deteriorates quality. Root crops keep best for storing in temperatures between 32° and 40° F. They require a bit of humidity, but if the storage area is too moist, sprouting will occur and the roots will become woody.

We do not grow turnips because my husband hates them, so we are free of the storage-odor problems characteristic of turnips. We store all of our root crops in layers in flat boxes in the unheated crawl space under the house. To hold moisture, I line and cover the storage boxes with the plastic bags that come from the cleaners, but such coverings must not be airtight or the roots will rot. Rotten roots smell worse than turnips.

Pumpkins and the hard-rind varieties of winter squash should be cut from the plants before heavy frost. Leave a piece of stem on each squash and store only perfect fruits. Both pumpkins and squash should be cured for about two weeks in heaps at the base of a tree or, if the weather is wet and cold, near the hot-water heater. A curing temperature of 75° F. will harden the skin and heal any cuts. The pumpkins and squash may then be stored in a cool (55° F.) dry place for two or three months. I have heard of rubbing warm paraffin into winter squash for keeping. To check black rot, my grandfather used to dip winter squashes in a formaldehyde solution just before storing. He used one part commercial formaldehyde to fifty parts water, and he disinfected the storage area with this solution, too.

A neighbor once told me about pumpkin wine, which I tried, but the pumpkin I chose was afflicted with pickle worm and the worm drank the wine. That must have been one pickled pickle worm because the dregs I tasted were rumlike and heavy. For pumpkin wine, simply cut the top off a small pumpkin as for a jack-o'-lantern, clean out the seeds and pack the topless pumpkin with brown sugar. Replace the top and seal it by dipping the whole sugar-packed pumpkin in paraffin. To do this, put hot water into a plastic bucket, melt paraffin and float it on top, and dip the pumpkin bottom first up to the lid. When the paraffin hardens on the fruit, drip paraffin around the replaced lid. Let the sealed pumpkin set for two months. If there is liquid left in it at that time, pour the wine into a sterilized bottle and bung the cork home.

North Carolina corncob jelly is a unique October product. If you have a farmer friend, mooch a dozen of the big, red, dried field-corn cobs. Crack the cobs into pieces, put them in a large pan and boil them with five pints of water. When the liquid has boiled down to three cups, strain it through a cloth and return the liquid to the fire. When boiling again, add one package of pectin and three cups of sugar; stir until dissolved, and boil until the mixture jells. Pour the boiling-hot jelly into hot, sterilized jars and seal with paraffin. Corncob jelly looks and tastes like a delicate apple jelly, and my husband says it is exactly right on French toast.

Tomatoes to be stored should be picked in October or before the first killing frost. Pick any stems from the tomatoes to keep them from puncturing each other. Before storing, wash the tomatoes and let them dry. (Rubbing off the dirt scars the skins and may cause decay.) Separate the tomatoes that show red from the robust green ones. Put any undersized tomatoes in a container for immediate cooking. Both the reddening tomatoes and the large green ones should be layered separately, one or two deep, in shallow boxes for ripening and covered or wrapped individually with newspaper.

Stored tomatoes should be checked once a week. If they are held at 44° F. in a somewhat moist, dark place, they will keep about six weeks. We have had fresh tomatoes ripen in storage for Christmas, but the keeping depends on the growing season, storage conditions and the variety of fruit.

Green tomatoes too small or damaged for winter storage make excellent chutneys, whole pickles and relishes, but I usually make green-tomato mincemeat.

For mincemeat, wash, drain, core and chop enough green

tomatoes to make six quarts of fruit. Sprinkle the green tomatoes with three tablespoons of salt and let them stand for one hour. Drain them, cover them with boiling water, and let them stand for five minutes, then drain a second time.

Put three whole oranges through the food chopper (medium blade).

Wash, drain, core and chop into thumbnail-sized pieces eight quarts of apples. I leave the skins on, although some people peel apples for mincemeat.

Mix the fresh fruit, including tomatoes, with three boxes of raisins, ten cups of sugar (half brown and half white), three tablespoons of cinnamon, one tablespoon each of cloves, nutmeg and ginger. Add one-and-a-half cups of vinegar and boil slowly until the tomatoes and apples are tender and the mincemeat takes on a thick, glossy consistency. Pour the boiling-hot mincemeat into hot, sterilized jars and seal. I process my quarts in a boiling-water bath for fifteen minutes; some people merely hot-seal pickle-type foods. That is, they fill the preheated jar with boiling produce and tighten the top. By vacuum action the jar seals itself.

A quart of green-tomato mincemeat bakes into a lusty pie, festive, yet filling enough to top off a supper of leftovers and entice everyone to smile.

The October earth is a storehouse of starchy wild roots. Cattails (*Typha Latifolia*), Arrowheads (*Sagittaria*), Daylily (*Hemerocallis fulva*), Alpine bistort (*Polygonum bistorta viviparum*), wild potato (*Psoralea esculenta*), evening primrose (*Oenothera biennis*), and Jerusalem artichoke (*Helianthus tuberosus*) all supply nutritious food for the digging. They may be used as potatoes or cooked as a turniplike vegetable.

One fresh October day in Virginia my daughter Penny and I went foraging for root crops near our cabin. In addition to a few evening primroses, which we hesitated to dig because their flowers were so cheerful, and a few dead members of the arum family, which we were afraid to dig because of shaky identification, we found a profusion of daylily tubers. The small roots are borne in large yellow clusters, and if the earth is moist, they are extremely simple to dig. We pulled the plants partway free from the soil, after shoving a spade underneath, and then we twisted off handfuls of the ropy roots. We popped each plant back into its hole, where it would live to bear more roots. Stealing daylily tubers does not seem to harm the plants. Penny and I washed the roots in a nearby creek, and within an hour we had a shopping bag full of clean tubers. At home we cooked part of them by cutting off the stringiest ends and boiling the middles in salted water for twenty minutes. Flavored with butter or cheese sauce, daylily roots are a pleasant starch-food substitute or vegetable.

Daylilies are one of the most versatile of food plants. In addition to the tubers, the sprouts, buds, flowers and dried flowers may be harvested with ease, and all are mild-tasting vegetables. Naturalized American plant citizens, daylilies, like many other naturalized Americans, give abundantly of themselves to their adopted country.

Although my grandfather used to state emphatically that "God created turnips to sweeten hog meat," and refused to eat them, he used to bring home baskets of wild potatoes, which he ate with relish. To me, they tasted like turnips. I have never dug the *Psoralea esculenta,* or prairie turnip, as my grandfather's wild potatoes were locally named, but I have eaten them prepared like potatoes. Found predominantly in the prairie states on the more arid parts of the great plains, the plants bear groups of three to five long cloverlike leaflets on a foot-tall hairy stalk, and the tight clusters of pealike flowers are bluish purple. Indians and pioneers are said to have eaten prairie turnips raw, baked and boiled, prepared in as many ways as potatoes. The globular turnip-shaped roots of wild potato are sweetest when found covered by turf; exposed, they turn bitter.

Although most plants used in flavoring are grown in herb gardens, there is no lack of wild seasonings available to a seasoned forager. Like cultivated culinary condiments, most wild spices may be used fresh or dried; leaves and flowers may be gathered in the summer, seeds collected before fall, and wild root condiments dug in early autumn.

Wild herbs should be clean before drying and thoroughly dried before storage. As with garden herbs, labeling of herbs should be done when they are put into sterilized, tightly covered keeping containers.

Leaf and flower herbs to be dried may be spread on screens in the shade and turned from time to time for three or four days, then oven-treated for ten minutes at as close to 100° F. as possible.

Some farm wives dry herbs by hanging them in the kitchen or attic for a week, then oven-treating them as above. Though a warm, dry, well-ventilated place may be used for indoor drying, all herbs should be dried quickly in order to retain color and oils.

In addition to drying herbs in the shade outdoors, or hanging them indoors, a third method that some people use is oven drying. Place the herbs on a cookie sheet in an oven for ten minutes with the heat turned on at the lowest possible temperature. Then turn off the heat and allow the herbs to dry in the oven. Straight oven drying may have to be repeated several times to insure that the herbs are fully dried. Dried herbs should not lose their color; this indicates a loss of fragrance and flavor.

Roots and bark require more time to dry than leaves. Roots should be washed, sliced, spread on a screen for about ten days and, when thoroughly dried, heated in a very low oven for twenty minutes before storing. Roots are usually brittle when dried.

Herb seeds should be dried on a paper and stirred to prevent molding, treated to a ten-minute stay in the oven at 100° F., then stored in a container with a tight lid.

Wild onions, garlic, chives and leek (*Allium*) leaves are gathered in spring and summer; the bulbs in fall may be used as substitutes for cultivated species. The *Allium* family may be used fresh or chopped and dried for winter use. I have frozen wild onions after chopping them and blanching them in boiling water.

The following wild plants may be used as herbs or condiments:

BAYBERRY (*Myrica pensylvanica*). Leaves may be used dried or fresh in soups as a substitute for bay leaves. Wax from the gray berries may be melted for candles. The beach shrub is boiled and cooled and the wax skimmed for use in dipping candles. Bayberry leaves on a pantry shelf are said to repel grain weevils.

CHECKERBERRY (*Gaultheria procumbens*). Winter-frosted berries and young leaves may be used fresh as a wintergreen flavoring. Mature leaves are dried for tea.

HORSE-RADISH (*Armoracia rorippa*). Fresh root may be grated into a peppery dressing. Dried root loses bite but may be used if desired.

JOHN-HENRY (*Tagetes minuta*). Young fresh leaves may be used in soups and meat dishes.

MINTS and horehound (*Labiatae*). Leaves may be used in flavoring sweets or in tea when both fresh and dried.

MUGWORT (*Artemisia vulgaris*). Leaves may be used in beverages, either as a fresh "sprig of bitters" or steeped from the dried leaves. Mugwort should be cut while flowering.

PEPPER-GRASS (*Lepidium*). Pods or seeds may be used as a pepper substitute or mixed with vinegar and used in marinating meat. Pepper-grass may be used dried or fresh.

SAMPIRE (*Salicornia*). Succulent young stems may be used as salt in salads when fresh. Indians dried sampire for use as a salt herb to be cooked with meat or greens.

SASSAFRAS (*Sassafras albidum*). Bark of the root may be used in candy flavoring when fresh or dried. Young leaves and stems may be used in broths, gumbos and soups. Sassafras roots may be eaten dried or fresh.

SMARTWEED (*Polygonum*). Leaves may be used fresh as a cayenne pepper substitute in eggs and salads. Dried seeds may be substituted for pepper.

SORREL (*Rumex*). Fresh leaves may be used as an acid seasoning for fish, salad or soup.

SPICEBUSH (*Lindera benzoin*). Dried young leaves and berries may be used as a substitute for allspice. Dried leaves are used as tea.

SWEET BIRCH (*Betula lenta*). Bark, young buds, leaves and twigs may be used either fresh or dried as an oil of wintergreen flavoring or as a delicate tea.

Sweet cicely (*Osmorhiza*). Root may be used as an anise flavoring when dried. Fresh leaves may be used in salad, and the fresh roots may be boiled like parsnips. Extreme care should be taken to identify correctly because this plant resembles poison hemlock.

Sweetgale (*Myrica gale*). Leaves may be used in sausage and meats as a fresh or dried sage substitute, or steeped in boiling water as an aromatic tea.

Tansy (*Tanacetum vulgare*). Young leaves may be used in eggs and salad for a fresh peppery flavor. Dried tansy (cut when flowering) may be used to flavor cream cheese.

Wild ginger (*Asarum canadense*). Dried root may be substituted for commercial ginger after it has been ground.

Wild edible nuts need little introduction. The well-known trees with their long, pinnately compounded leaves, squiggly flowers and husk-covered nuts grow from the Mississippi Valley eastward. Black walnuts and hickory nuts are the most abundant throughout the central and eastern states; pecans range from Indiana southward and butternuts are found farther north into southern Canada.

Early settlers relied on nuts to supplement winter food, eating them raw or dried and ground into flour. Pickling butternuts was also a European-American custom. Half-grown softish, unhusked nuts were first boiled, then reboiled in salted water until the water remained clear and the nuts became tender. They were soaked in cold, fresh water for two days (the water changed two times a day), drained, dried and placed between alternating layers of pickling spices— cloves, mace, cinnamon bark, pepper and salt—in a crock and covered with boiling vinegar. The crock was covered and placed in a cool, dark place, and the nuts were not eaten until the new year.

Nutting parties traditionally searched the woods each fall for fallen nuts or walnuts clinging to trees. Indians, however, were more devious. They observed where squirrels hid their caches and then raided. The Indians used nuts as nibbles; they made flour and pemmican-type cakes from nutmeats;

they used mashed nuts in gravies and soups; and nut oil was used as a food lubricant.

To extract the meats, the nuts were pounded until finely cracked. Next they were slowly boiled in water. Within several hours the nut oil floated and was skimmed from the surface. Waterlogged shells sank, and between the sunken shells and floating oil the nutmeats swam. These were ladled out of the pot and mashed into nutmeat cakes. Sun-dried cakes were saved for winter along with the oil, which was used as a butter and animal-fat substitute. To reconstitute nut cakes for use in soup and bread, or as a vegetable, the cakes were simmered in water.

Nut oil rapidly becomes rancid and deteriorates in a warm place; but if kept cool, it retains its sweet clarity for six months.

Every year our family tries to beat the squirrels to local nuts, and nearly every year we fail. We sometimes manage to pick up a bushel or so, however, and successful or not, nutting on a Sunday afternoon is always an adventure. Scuffling through leaves, moist earth-smells rising, a hustling wind worrying the grasses, the sun's warm cheek lingering on south slopes, all mingle with silent goodbyes and thank-yous to the autumn woodland.

At home we cover the walnuts with screens so the suburban squirrels will keep their paws out of them. When the husks are brittle we clean them and lay them again under screening to dry. In about two weeks our son Martin cracks the heavy black shells and we all sit and watch television while picking the meats, which will be used in fruitcakes and cookies.

As October evenings lengthen and the fire invites us indoors, our girls ask if they can make candy. Fudge, taffy, divinity with nuts—a bite of sweet goes well after supper and when homework is done.

Wild foods offer their own gift to the sweet tooth. We used

to gather the white woolly horehound mint (*Labiatae marrubium*) and boil a potful of leaves, dried or fresh, into a strong tea. To one-quarter cup of the strained tea we'd add one pound of brown sugar. After stirring over a low heat until the sugar was dissolved, we boiled the liquid until a hard ball was formed. (The hard-ball test was passed when a little of the syrup, dropped into a teacup of cold water, formed a brittle, hard ball.) We then mixed in a tablespoon of vinegar, boiled the candy up once more and poured it immediately into a well-buttered platter. When the horehound brittle was cold we slid it onto wax paper and broke it with a hammer.

I like spearmint candy made in the same manner; but with strong tea of spearmint (*Mentha spicata*) white sugar is used instead of brown.

Wintergreen candy is a favorite with most youngsters, and an extract may be made from checkerberries (*Gaultheria procumbens*) or their leaves. Berries are gathered in the early fall, but if the dried leaves are preferred, they should be picked and dried in the spring while they are still tender and filled with oil. Steep the checkerberries or their leaves in boiling water, or boil if necessary, until three tablespoons of strong tea are secured. Add two cups of brown sugar and stir until the sugar is dissolved. Boil the syrup until it tests for a hard ball. Add one tablespoon of vinegar to the syrup, boil for one minute more and pour it into a well-buttered platter. When cold, break the candy into small pieces.

We made hard candy once or twice a year when I was growing up, and the spicy nibbles added variety to our lives when we pulled it into taffy. For pulled taffy we buttered our hands, and just as the candy was beginning to harden on the platter, we cut a hunk, found a partner with buttered hands, and pulled until the sweet became airy, light-colored and hard. The key to pulling taffy into light tubes of goodness is to start pulling when it is almost too hot to handle; taffy pullers have to move fast to keep from burning themselves. Each partner would pull, fold over the candy, and pull again.

193

I remember one girl who had to cut her hair when someone mixed her pigtail with the taffy. Although mint taffy is a taste change, sorghum or corn-syrup taffy was more popular with my friends.

Crystallized ginger root is a wonderful sweet. Too much ginger is said to cause jackleg, that characteristic stumbling walk of chronic alcoholics. As a nibble or eaten in moderate quantities, candied wild ginger rivals the Oriental confection. Syrupy candied ginger root makes a bitey meat relish.

Wild ginger (*Asarum canadense*) grows in rich woods from Virginia to Minnesota on a low plant with root cords growing from a knotty but superficial root. The leaves are heart-shaped, mottled green, two or three inches in diameter, leathery in texture, and grow on tough, hairy stalks. During April and May a reddish-brown cup-shaped flower with three lobes blooms at ground level and emerges between two leafstalks.

Ginger root may be dug at any time and dried, but in October the roots are full and are better for candied ginger. The leaves turn rusty before frost and are easily spotted. The rootstock may simply be washed and then dried in a very low oven or laid on a kitchen shelf where the air can circulate.

To candy ginger, I cut the dry roots into short pieces (or manageable strings if they are thin), cover them with water and boil them slowly until they are tender. I drain the ginger root and cool it in a colander. Using equal measures of root and white sugar, I put the ingredients into a large heavy pot, add just enough water to moisten the sugar, and boil it slowly, stirring often until the sugar dissolves, then occasionally until the ginger becomes somewhat clear and the liquid has nearly boiled away. (If I want syrupy relish, I spoon some ginger and juice into a jar at this time.) For ginger-root candy I lower the fire and stir the crystallized root continually. When it is practically dry, I turn off the fire and spoon several pieces at a time into a brown-paper bag containing one-half cup of white sugar. I shake the bag and with a slotted spoon remove the hot, sugared root to wax paper. I repeat the process until all of the root is sugared. A pint or so in the jar at the back of the cabinet will last all winter for nibbles. It is not the kind of candy to eat by handfuls.

Cranberries (*Vaccinium vitis-idaea* or *V. oxycoccus*), the northland's contribution to autumn sweets, are tart berries familiar to nearly everyone. After frost has sweetened their dispositions they may be boiled into a sauce, jelly, juice, pie, a whipped dessert, a spiced relish, or brewed into wine.

Cranberry wine is beautiful and it tastes better than its look-alike, beet wine.

Put a gallon of berries in a large enamel pot with a gallon of water and cook until the berries pop, but do not allow them to come to a full boil. Stir in five cups of sugar and a box of raisins, turn off the fire and set aside. When the wine mixture reaches room temperature, add a package of yeast dissolved in a cup of warm water, cover and allow it to ferment in the enamel pot. Mix and squeeze the fruit with your hands every day. In two weeks' time, strain, cover, and allow the wine to work for one more week.

Carefully siphon the wine into sterilized bottles and cap or cork lightly. Cranberry wine has a tendency to be a "long worker," so do not bung home the cork tightly until all action has stopped; then seal each bottle with paraffin and save the wine for next Thanksgiving. Cranberry wine, like a bitter-sweet memory, tugs at the heart with its beauty and adds a tart fullness to a meal.

Persimmons are another soul food for foragers. *Diospyros virginiana*, a temperate-zone member of the ebony family, is found from Connecticut to Florida and from Missouri southward. The golden fruits are puckery before they ripen, but they sweeten as the sun holds them on the tree until frost. To gather persimmons, we usually wait until an early-morning frost firms the fruit; then we spread a sheet and shake the tree.

Pudding, custard, pie, bread, wine, beer: ingenious minds

have created numerous persimmon happinesses.

We love persimmon pudding. Sometimes I steam it and poke a sprig of holly into the pudding ball for holiday cheer.

Usually I bake small loaf puddings. They keep well in the refrigerator and I often slice them as a moist cakelike treat for school lunches.

Mash enough fluid-ripe persimmons through a colander for two cups of pulp. Mix in two cups of sugar, two eggs, one cup of milk, two teaspoons of cinnamon and one teaspoon of salt. If I have raisins, dates or nuts, I add one cupful, together with four teaspoons of melted butter, two cups of flour, and four teaspoons of baking soda. Mix all ingredients well, divide into buttered bread pans and bake at 350°F. for about an hour. When it is done, the pudding pulls away from the pan and has turned a glossy ebony brown. My family enjoys warm pudding with cream, or cold pudding with a hunk of hard sauce.

Persimmon wine is something else! From our experience, you have to be fast and covetous to get any when serving it to a group.

For persimmon wine, lay four or five six-inch boughs of pine in the bottom of a ten-gallon crock. Add eight mashed sweet potatoes, washed and boiled but unpeeled, a box of raisins and about a peck of unseeded but mashed persimmons. Cover with two or three gallons of warm water and stir in five pounds of sugar. Add a package of dry yeast dissolved in a cup of warm water with a teaspoon of sugar, and fill the crock with warm water to within four inches of the top. Cover and let set.

Persimmon wine requires five or six weeks for complete fermentation. All the garbage will float and you will have to peep below the debris to see the action. When fermentation stops, strain through several cloths, allow liquid to settle for two days, and siphon the wine into sterilized bottles. Cork lightly, because this brew is untrustworthy. When the corks stay down, seal each bottle with paraffin. Three years is the longest we have been able to keep persimmon wine, but we have found that as it ages it mellows into champagnelike smoothness and takes on a bouquet of the autumn woods.

Libra has been called hunter's moon. Although my husband and I no longer hunt, we sometimes use hunting as an excuse to tramp through the woods. We love to eat game, however, and from my grandparents I learned that half the success of game cookery depends upon the handling of the meat.

Game should be bled and cleaned immediately after killing. Believe this dumb hunter who says from experience that there is no ickier, colder job than eviscerating a stone-cold moose. (Once, consumed by pride, I flew back to town, ostensibly to gather supplies but in reality to tell the news of my first moose kill. Four hours later, back at the carcass in the stinking cold, I suffered as only one up to his armpit inside a frigid moose can suffer.)

As soon as it has been shot, most game should be bled by cutting the neck under the chin through to the bone. If possible it should be hung by the back legs for bleeding, or at least the head of the animal should be lower than the rest of the carcass.

Some people skin small game before removing the entrails; however, if preferred, the hide may be left on to protect the meat from dirt. Large animals should be cooled quickly and the carcass should be propped open to permit air to circulate. Whether the hide is left on or removed, all game should be eviscerated as soon as possible after killing. I have found that the excitement of the hunt is still very much alive for some time after the killing, and as your mind relives the experience, field dressing is accomplished with little conscious effort.

When dealing with small animals, the hunter must always be aware of musk glands. Groundhog, muskrat, beaver, raccoon, porcupine and opossum contain orange to cream-colored, waxy, bean-shaped glands under each foreleg. They must be searched for, or felt with the fingertips, and removed without breaking. On most small game a second pair of musk glands is found high in the small of the back. However, the muskrat and beaver carry their second pair of glands under each hind leg. To ensure good meat, the musk must be removed along with all visible fat—fat on game often tastes strong.

Some people soak their small-game meat in salt water or in vinegar-salt water for twenty-four hours. One-half cup of salt mixed with one cup of vinegar to six quarts of water is said to remove the wild taste and to tenderize the meat. One woodsman I knew simply covered the cleaned game with cold water and let it stand two or three days.

My grandmother used to remove the fat, wash the game, rub it with baking soda, cover with water, and let it stand in the soda water for two days. Sometimes she marinated game overnight in vinegar before changing the soaking liquid to water and olive oil. Once I tried both procedures on a geriatric squirrel. The treatment foamed and frothed so, I thought the squirrel had a delayed rabies reaction. As matters turned out, I cremated that poor aged creature under the broiler and never knew whether the foam tenderized the meat or not.

In general the rules for small game preparation are simple:
1. Bleed well.
2. Eviscerate and remove all musk glands.
3. Remove all fat.
4. Soak (cold water, salt water, salt-vinegar water, or rub with soda and cover with water).
5. Add fat in cooking.

Most game birds of unknown vintage should be treated with one of the soak techniques and simmered for one hour before browning. Soaked and simmered before use in a gourmet recipe, fowl such as mud hens, mergansers, fish ducks and rook all can be inspired to tease your palate.

I have cooked fool hens, or grouse, on the trail and coots on the beach. Enjoyment of less-than-genteel game boils down to how hungry you are. The coot tasted like tough cod-liver oil, and the fool hen grew bigger the longer it was chewed. However, if I had to cook either in the kitchen, I would try soaking and simmering prior to braising or to the creation of coot stew.

Beaver, if young and virgin, is a delicacy like moist, dark turkey thighs, but some senior citizens of the beaver clan turn out to be enormous hunks of coarse meat. I knew a miner who also trapped near Eagle, Alaska, and who ground beaver, added salt pork, and made sausage which he stuffed into gauze sleeves and smoked over alder. I was cooking at a neighboring camp and I helped him with the sleeves but never tasted his beaver sausage. He hated women.

Some river people rejoice over beaver tails. The tail hide, like turtle skin, loosens readily after a momentary plunging into boiling water, or by laying the tail on hot rocks near the campfire (the odor of scorched beaver tail is not recommended, however). After skinning, pot-roasted beaver tail, with sauerkraut and potatoes popped into the pan during the last hour, is good. The meat has a gristly, chewy consistency and a sweet fresh-pork flavor.

Beavers sometimes run to thirty-five or forty pounds, and fine roasts and stews come from a single eager beaver. Like most of God's creatures, we are a product of that which we eat. Fish-eating bears taste fishy and jack-pine-eating beavers taste jacky. The vinegar-water overnight soaking removes some of the pine-pitch taste, liberating the beaver from his fat removes some more, and jack beaver eaten with a forkful of cranberry sauce eliminates the jack altogether.

In Virginia, the training of dogs to trail coon is often considered more important than hunting for food. My husband and I have sat on the cabin porch in the darkness and listened to the hounds along the ridge or near the river. People who run hounds understand their cries, and they hunt with their ears. We try to guess whether the coon has been treed or whether it has tricked its pursuers. I often suffer quick stabs of sympathy for the ringtail.

"The moon has to be just right for good coon hunting," a young mountain friend told us. "Bright moon spooks coon; wind does, too."

Sometimes the hunters follow their hounds, but more often they turn the dogs loose and sit swapping tales and interpreting the sounds of the hunt. Most raccoons give dogs a good run, then head for water and escape; some confuse the dogs by starting to climb a tree, then jumping wide, but other raccoons tree. When the hounds trap a coon in a treetop, they circle and bay. This particular cry calls their master, who spotlights the coon, and if he wants meat, he either shoots or shakes the masked mammal from his refuge.

Coon hunting is a satisfying sport, an audio love affair between droop-eyed, long-eared hounds and a woodsman, a primitive chase that spiritually returns the hunter to the natural world of night.

Coons love to eat corn and crawdaddies; they are considered "clean" game, and roasted with sweet potatoes, dotted with butter, there is no more gentle-tasting meat.

Most small game require fat to lubricate the meat and enhance its flavor, and muskrat is no exception. On the Koyukok River in Alaska, Indians of the interior traditionally traded caribou hides and wolverine fur with northern tribesmen for salt and seal oil. The mild deer-meat flavor of muskrat is accentuated by the taste of the sea that a seal-oil dressing adds. Many Indians used seal oil as a body cream, a lotion, an outboard-motor oil, a leather softener, a sled-runner grease, a laxative and a hair tonic. Many native homes are permeated with the odor. I find seal-oil smells as comforting as woodfire smoke or the hushed sweetness of a cosmetics counter in a department store.

After cleaning and skinning muskrat and removing fat and musk glands, this red meat may be fricasseed or stewed like a hen, or it may be fried, kabobed or ground into muskburgers, first adding lubricating fat such as lard or seal oil, if you like.

Next to deer and rabbit, squirrels must be the most popular small game. There are abundant nut trees and thus abundant nutty squirrels on our Culpeper County place. One fall, when our children were small, we decided to give them a practical lesson in pioneer living. With a magnificent shot into the branchy Virginia pines, Lewis brought down a squirrel near the cabin. The weather was cold, so I lined up the children inside at a window where they could see, and I began to skin the squirrel outside.

Three little rosy-cheeked youngsters staring at Mommy. Then there were two. Finally only Martin stood firm. The girls lay sobbing in their beds. I think the lesson came on a little strong.

Surprisingly, the children ate and enjoyed that squirrel stew and they still look forward to squirrel each fall. Squirrel, along with rabbit, seldom requires soaking and simmering first. I prepare them as I cook chicken.

Traditionally the hunt has satisfied man's basic needs of response, recognition, new experience and security. The hunter was loved because he provided for his family. He received recognition through his skill as a hunter. Each hunt was a new experience and food was basic to security. Today our culture fulfills these needs in different ways. However, many men still hunt. These men reach back into the traditions of October and with ritualized discipline seek out the exhilarating challenge and rewards of the hunt. They walk through the mature and splendid season watching, hearing, smelling, feeling. The tensions of crowded living leave them and a natural pulse is renewed.

XI

Freeze-up
NOVEMBER

Frustrated Scorpio. Mulch garden, cut hardwoods for grafting. Late greens and fresh fish. "Perry." Deer hunters and venison; mincemeat. Sagittarius heralds butchering season: slaughter, scald; carcass cleaned, cut up. Pork: dry sugar-cure method, packing, overhauling, drying bacon, sausage making, canning sausage. Lard making, crackling bread. Soap making. Variety meats: headcheese, scrapple, spicy times in November.

Sᴌᴏᴡ ᴛᴏ sᴛᴏʀᴍ, slow to warm; watery, fruitful, feminine, Scorpio (October 23 to November 22) seems to hold a grudge because its weather is neither autumn nor winter. Though the moon is passing through its fruitful sign, the sun does not cooperate and the frustrated Scorpion escapes into a dreamy, misanthropic existence.

Gardening grinds to a stop.

But straw should be heaped on strawberries, leaves should be layered on parsnips, and mulch should be applied to the perennial herbs. If roots for forcing into greens are to be lifted, they should be put into sandboxes in the cellar.

Although the moon appears indifferent, there is one positive job to accomplish in November. Moon-sign watchers declare that the propagation of hardwoods is best done on the growing moon under Scorpio. Hardwood cuttings from all kinds of deciduous trees and shrubs, as well as evergreens, yews, boxwood and hollies may be made during this fruitful, watery sign. The slips should be tied into bundles and kept in damp sand in a cool, dark place. In February or March, while the moon is passing through the moist sign of Pisces, cuttings should be planted outdoors in rooting sand (optimumly when the moon is in the first quarter).

Foraging slacks off in November, but if you are lucky, you will have located a protected sunny slope where dock, lamb's-quarters and other spring greens push forth new growth in the lull between first frosts and freeze-up. We have such a spot above the cabin glen, and though most wild foods are entering hibernation, we sometimes enjoy greens for Thanksgiving.

Fishing for the table generally starts slowing down this

time of year, too, but some fish don't know that they are supposed to seek deep water and sleep.

Bluegills or perch are usually hungry the last few weeks
before freeze-up, and earthworms are their favorite bedtime
snack. On a bright fall day, pick a moist, humus-laden spot
and drive a stake four or five inches into the ground. With the
back of the hammer rub the wood so that it gives off dry
grunts and calls up fishing worms. The curious or frightened
creatures will obligingly come out of the ground.

After wild foods have been gathered and the garden has
been set by, a brisk walk to the river and wetting a line gives
a rational excuse for wilderness prowling. Though scorned by
some epicurean sophisticates, the lowly perch-type pan fish,
rolled in cornmeal and fried until golden in sweet oil, com-
pliments late wild greens.

Each fall my grandmother culled pears and made a wine
which she called "perry" from the ripe but imperfect fruit.

After cutting out all seeds and bad spots, she chopped the
washed but unpeeled pears, covered them with an equal volume of water and boiled them slowly for not more than ten
minutes. She poured the pears and juice into a crock, added
three pounds of sugar to each gallon of fruit and stirred until
the sugar was dissolved. A box of raisins and a sliced lemon
were dropped into the wine, and when it cooled to lukewarm
she added one cake of yeast which had been dissolved in one
cup of warm water. The crock was covered and the wine allowed to ferment for three weeks. The mixture was strained
and the liquid siphoned into sterilized bottles and corked
lightly. When fermentation stopped, she decanted each bottle
of "green perry" into a clean bottle, leaving the sediment,
then filled each new bottle of wine with a strong liquor such
as brandy.

The bottles were sealed and stored until "a year from
Steve's birthday" (December 26), when we all toasted my
grandfather's health. I do not know for sure, but I suspect

they toasted Steve's well-being at other times too, because that was great wine.

In some parts of our country "getting your deer" each autumn is as accepted a custom as getting a new dress each Eastertime. Hunters study maps, talk with friends, scout and prepare their equipment as carefully as a promenader creates her spring wardrobe.

In the dark, cold silence of predawn, hunters stand blending with the woods. Deer are nocturnal feeders, and the hunters wait noiselessly for "their buck" to browse into view. Though chilled and stiff, every waiting hunter feels a hum of excitement as the sky lightens and movement becomes visible. Deer usually switch their tails before raising their heads while feeding, and flicking white tails signal the dawn and rifle shots.

Some hunters prefer to "jump" or stalk their trophy. Wind in their faces, they search low for droppings or freshly cropped twigs. Other shots rip the wild stillness and the season of venison-meat cookery begins.

Fatless venison steaks, marinated for two hours in olive oil and lemon juice, broiled over hot coals, turned frequently until ruddy brown, sprinkled over with paprika, pepper and salt, daubed with butter, and eaten in a cozy cabin, are unequivocally recommended.

The cardinal rule of game cooking is: *Think tough!* Most wild meats are tough and should be marinated if not cooked a long time with moist heat.

Venison may be seasoned, then wrapped in buttered paper or muslin and poached in a shallow pan with one inch of water; it may be dabbed with butter and roasted in a tightly covered pan, or it may be seasoned, sealed in a flour-and-water paste and baked. Whichever way large pieces of venison are cooked, one-half hour before serving, the meat should be removed from its covering and then baked uncovered and basted to bring out its bloom of color and flavor.

I usually season venison with bacon because the fat pork restores oil to the meat as well as adding a smoke flavor. I cover a six-to-ten-pound roast of venison with bacon strips, then bake in a closed container in moist heat for four to five hours at 325° F. I uncover the meat and baste during the last half-hour in a 375° F. oven. Either the meat juices or dry sherry are suitable for basting.

After removing the fat, venison may be handled and preserved by any of the common meat-curing methods. Canned venison is excellent. Salted and smoked venison is a treat, like smoked turkey. Salted and dried venison, though tough and chewy, is remarkably filling and is good if the nibbles are cut small enough. Venisonburgers are an excellent way to use tough meat. Twice-ground venison sausage, flavored with one-eighth cup of ground salt pork to two cups of ground venison, one teaspoon each of sage and salt, and one-eighth teaspoon of pepper, is a gastronomic delight. Venison stew, made with your favorite beef-stew recipe, but with a small can of sliced pineapple added a moment before thickening, is a happy variation for cooking old deer. Of course, barbecued deer meat served over heaps of rice or on heated hamburger rolls is a campfire specialty. Venison ragouts, casseroles with noodles, and jars of jellied cold meat all entice the taste buds.

My grandmother used to put up a half-dozen quarts of venison mincemeat every year. She boiled two or three pounds of fatless, tough pieces of deer meat in apple cider to cover until tender; then she chopped the meat in a food grinder with about one pound of store-bought suet. She washed, cored and chopped (skins on) twelve pounds of red apples and two whole oranges, and the fruit, venison and suet were returned to the cider to cook. A quart and a half more cider was added along with two boxes of raisins, one box of currants, two pounds of brown sugar, two tablespoons of cinnamon, one tablespoon each of allspice and salt, two teaspoons of nutmeg, one teaspoon of cloves and one-half teaspoon of ginger. The mincemeat was simmered for about an hour or until it became thick and brown. It was stirred frequently during the final thirty minutes and the exquisite smells of the kitchen during mincemeat making were enough to make eyes grow watery with emotion. My grandmother packed the hot mincemeat into hot, sterilized jars, sealed them, and processed the quarts for three hours in a boiling-water bath. She cautioned that, because of the meat, the quarts should be processed a long time.

Grandaddy considered mincemeat pie without two or three jiggers of blackberry brandy added just before the top crust was put on to be a violation of the rights of man.

"Men haven't many God-given rights," Uncle Steve would address the company at the table, "but he does have the right to die, to pay taxes, and the right to have blackberry brandy in his holiday pie." Grandaddy's generous nose would sniff the mincemeat affectionately as he paused, knife poised, ready to cut.

The constellation Scorpio ends its disenchanted reign on November 22, when Sagittarius (November 22 to December 22) takes over. With the fiery, dry, barren and masculine characteristics of the Bowman, eloquent harmony returns to the zodiac.

Sagittarius apparently is the most favorable sign under which to butcher. For best keeping characteristics, meat should be slaughtered during the waning moon, with the fourth quarter a superior time to salt and smoke pork. Moon followers say that meat spits in the pan and bacon curls if it has been slaughtered during the waxing quarters, and if it has been killed during the moist zodiac sign. They say it will not keep well.

Butchered by the moon or not, prior to slaughter hogs should be taken off feed for twenty-four hours, given lots of water and kept from becoming excited. Because butchering is heavy, hard, stinking work, it is best done cooperatively. In

Missouri, several neighbors used to butcher on the same day, and they cooperated by sharing tools and muscles. I remember one old gent who got tanked and shot off a poor hog's ear. With a shattering squeal, the animal rammed through the fence and was sprinting down the road before any of the cooperating butchers realized what had happened.

Most hogs are stuck, that is, they are hung by the hind foot and the slaughterman severs an artery in the neck while a second man holds the animal. We recently purchased a hog that was so mean no one could get close, so it was shot first and moments later an incision made in the throat in front of the breastbone, to insure a good bleed.

Scalding in 150° F. water with a little lye or wood ashes follows. After scalding and scraping, the carcass is scrubbed clean.

Next, the hog is hung by the tendons, the head is cut off, the carcass is split, the entrails removed, the backbone is sawed lengthwise to the shoulders. When this is done, the men disappear to wash and grab a nip, while the women "fist" out the leaf lard, or pull the warm white leaf fat from the carcass; then they free the liver and heart, strip and wash casings (if these are to be saved), and remove the darker ruffle fat for soap grease. The carcass is transported to its owner's house for chilling overnight, the area cleaned, and a second hog is slaughtered.

I lived in one community where neighbors slaughtered eight hogs in one day. By the time they got around to the last hog, one man ended up in the slushy, scalding tank, two were fighting over whose liver belonged to whom, the butchers were axing the backbone, and someone stole the tenderloins.

Trimming and cutting the carcass is an individual family task. When thoroughly cool, the carcass is sawed through the third and fourth ribs at right angles to the backbone, the jowl trimmed to be saved for bacon, the neck bones severed and trimmed for sausage meat, and the shanks removed. The hams, pork loins, ribs and belly meat are separated and trimmed and the trimmings saved for sausage and lard.

Meat curing may be defined as the addition of salt (*sodium chloride*), saltpeter (*sodium nitrate*), sugar and spices for the purpose of preserving. Salt inhibits the growth of microorganisms in meat, and flavors it and influences tenderness. Sugar reduces the harshness of the salt, flavors pork, and colors cooked meat. Saltpeter assists in the curing process and in holding the color of uncooked meat. Sometimes pork is smoked after salting, which dries, seals and flavors the meat.

Fresh pork does not improve with age; after it has been thoroughly chilled, it should be kept refrigerated and should be processed within five days.

Most people I know "sugar cure," or dry cure, by rubbing the meat surface with salt, sugar and saltpeter and pumping a liquid mixture of these ingredients, called pickle, into the larger pieces. The cure-rubbed or pickle-pumped hams and bacon are placed into a crock or barrel to cure, one-and-a-half to three days to the pound, depending upon the size of the piece and the recipe.

My grandparents used to say it took eight months to flavor a fifteen-pound ham because the salt, sugar and nitrate had to penetrate through the fat and fibers into the deep muscles; then the ham had to age by hanging.

Sausage, variety meats and bacon cure more quickly, and by the same token their quality deteriorates before the larger, longer-cured pieces.

Meat to be cured should be kept cold but not frozen; it should be weighed and the curing ingredients measured. Too much salt makes the meat dry and overly salty to taste. Too little salt encourages spoilage. Too much saltpeter toughens meat. The length of time hams and bacons are to be kept in cure should be figured out and marked on the calendar. Two or three days to the pound for ham and one-and-one-half days to the pound for bacon is average.

If you wish to dry-cure pork, the trimmed hams, bacons and shoulders should be weighed, and for every hundred pounds of meat, dry-mix eight pounds of coarse-ground plain salt with two pounds of sugar and two ounces of saltpeter. It is important to mix the ingredients thoroughly.

Divide the curing mixture into two parts and save one part for resalting when the hams are overhauled at a later time.

Rub one part of the sugar-cure mix into all surfaces of the hams, making sure to poke some into the ends along the bone. Rubbing in the cure should be done with a slow, kneading motion, being careful not to roughen the surface on the flesh side. Press the curing mixture firmly onto all surfaces and carefully fit the salted meat, skin side down, into a clean crock or plastic container.

The bigger the piece of meat, the more curing mixture should be rubbed into and patted onto it. Conversely, bacon and small cuts of pork utilize only a sprinkling of dry cure, but it should be rubbed well into the meat. A thin covering of salt cure is patted on each piece and the bacons should be fitted, skin side down, on top of the hams in the crock. Keep the bacon slabs as flat as possible and press the top piece, skin side up, against the other meat. A layer of curing mixture should coat the top piece.

Firm pressure on the meat by means of a weighted lid insures a finer cure. I use plastic gallon milk cartons filled with cold water to hold our pork in cure, and we cure in a large plastic trash can.

The meat should be held in a cool (38° to 48° F.) bug-free place and covered with a cloth during the specified period of cure.

Hams and larger pieces of pork should be resalted or overhauled every seven to ten days during the cure process. Using the second half of the sugar-salt curing mixture, each ham or large piece of pork is rubbed and bare spots are covered. Changing the position of the pieces during overhaul insures a more uniform cure. Pack the remainder of the curing mixture around the big pieces, but add no more curing mixture to the bacon.

Techniques and ingredients in meat curing vary, but do not be afraid to give the salt plenty of time to work. Temperature also affects curing time required; in cold weather a longer curing time is needed, and in higher temperatures fats tend to become rancid if the amount of salt is not adequate. Meats must be watched and times adjusted to the individual piece.

After the specified time in cure is completed, wash the meat in lukewarm water. Soak the bacons for thirty minutes and the hams an hour. Scrub off the salt and grease. Hang the meat in a cool, dry place and let it drain. It may take a week to dry the cured meat.

When the sugar-salt-cured pork is thoroughly dry, wrap each piece in muslin and then in several pieces of heavy brown paper. Finally, place each wrapped ham, bacon and shoulder in a grocery bag to secure it against insects. Each sack of meat is hung in the cool, dark basement.

Cured meat may be eaten immediately or held a year or more before cutting.

Some people use commercial sugar-salt cure, which often contains flavoring such as smoke or pepper. Commercial salt-cure products are extremely simple to apply and they usually produce a tasty, uniform cure.

After the larger pieces of pork and bacon have been put down into the pickle barrel, farmers make fresh sausage from the scrap pieces and parts trimmed from the hams and sides. There are as many recipes for making sausage as there are people who make it.

Most sausage contains one-third fat and two-thirds lean, ground through the coarse plate of the grinder and seasoned and ground a second time through the fine plate. Sage, salt and pepper are traditionally used as seasonings for fresh sausage; omit sage when freezing.

My grandmother used to put down ten pounds of trimmings ground twice with four tablespoons of salt, three tablespoons of sage, five teaspoons of pepper, one tablespoon of sugar, one and one-half teaspoons of cloves and one teaspoon of nutmeg.

She sometimes bought casings from the butcher, who made them out of intestines, but more often she boiled muslin and sewed it into bags two and a half inches in diameter and fifteen feet long. One time she was saving money and she boiled one of Grandaddy's white shirts which he claimed had grown too small. As it turned out, she had cut up his church shirt, and when we ate that sausage, Grandaddy asked if he was eating from the neck or the tail.

With today's ease of freezing bulk meat, few people case fresh sausage; but if it is to be put into casings, they should be stuffed immediately after grinding the meat. Before using salted natural pork casings, they should be soaked for several minutes in warm water and rinsed; muslin casings should be moistened. The sausage should be soft enough to stuff tightly so that no air pockets will form. Some sausage makers knead their sausage for thirty or forty minutes to soften it before stuffing.

Many sausage grinders are equipped with stuffers over which the casings are pulled and fed out as the casings are filled. Ends should be tied tightly and the bags dipped into paraffin or melted lard to seal the surfaces. Unless the sausage is to be smoked (which is done before the paraffin dip), cased sausages should be refrigerated or frozen.

One year we were threatened with beetles and mites that infest meats, so Grandma canned fresh sausage. Because canning changes the flavor of spices, she seasoned the sausage lightly and omitted the sage. She made the ground meat into patties and fried them until they were light brown. She packed the hot sausage patties into hot pint jars, filled each to within one inch from the top, and poured some grease from the skillet into each jar. The jars were sealed and processed in a boiling-water bath for three hours. Pressure cookers are recommended for canning meats because of the inordinate length of time required to destroy bacteria in meats. Canned sausage is a mild yet intense meat-flavored surprise. One of the most versatile and eagerly sought after pork products, it may be spiced, baked with wine, or simply fried for a quick and tempting meal.

After the hams and bacon have been put in the cure, and the sausage made and frozen or cased, the rendering of creamy white lard is the next chore of butchering. Lard should be made as soon as possible after slaughtering because air deteriorates pork fat.

Lard making was a point of honor among pioneer women; high-quality lard was needed in baking and in the preparation of wild game. Lard was often used to moisten venison. Even when commercially butchered meat was available, poor refrigeration let fat become rancid so that it had to be removed before cooking. Lard replaced the trimmed fat. Lard and oil were held in higher esteem in early-day cooking than they are in today's world of marbled, tender, well-refrigerated meat.

Leaf fat, back fat, and belly trimmings are usually cut into three-quarter-inch pieces and rendered together for lard. Because of the fire hazard, most people who butcher their own meat prefer to render lard out-of-doors. We know several families who build a fire the day they butcher, clean their three-legged, round-bottomed lard kettles, pour a quart of water into them and toss in the chunked fat as it is removed from the pig. Throughout the day steam rises from the rendering fat, and between other butchering chores, the lard kettles are stirred and wood is added to the fire. Lard must not scorch, nor must it just lie there and not cook. It should melt and boil gently. Cracklings (the cooked skin and tissue) will float and brown and then sink to the bottom. After the cracklings begin to sink, the lard must be stirred constantly. When the cracklings sink, a sliced potato is often tossed into the kettle to purify the lard. Some people add a teaspoon of baking soda to the nearly rendered lard for whitening. When completely melted, the lard is dipped into cans or other unbreakable containers, covered tightly and stored in a cool dark place.

The danger of being burned during lard dipping is great. I knew a woman whose leg was drawn up behind her from lard-burn scars; I once taught a child who had lost a hand when hot lard had spilled on her.

With proper care, lard rendering, poking the fire, stirring, nibbling the hot cracklings can be a pleasant chore.

If you make lard, crackling cornbread is a must. After the lard is drawn off, the best cracklings are salvaged, poured with grease into hot, sterilized jars, and sealed. Sealing the jars will keep them fresh, and crackling cornbread may be made throughout the winter.

Stir together one-and-a-half cups of corn meal, one-half cup of flour, two teaspoons of baking powder, one tablespoon of sugar and one-half teaspoon of salt. Rub in one-half cup of larded cracklings; take handfuls of the dry ingredients and rub them together with the cracklings until they are moist with grease. When the cornbread mixture is lumpy, but well mixed, add one egg and one-and-one-half cups of milk. Stir only until it is mixed and pour the lumpy cornbread into a greased eight-by-ten-inch pan. Bake in a hot oven, 450° F., for twenty to thirty minutes or until golden brown. Crackling cornbread, eaten hot with creamed country sausage and beans, or with kielbasa and sauerkraut, or oozing with tart apple jelly, is a long remembered treat.

Making soap is another butchering chore. After the lard has been rendered, the off-color ruffle fat or entangled trim, the leftover drippings, and the heavy bottom cracklings are gathered for soap. The ruffle fat is rendered separately. Next, the refuse fats and crackling sludge are put into a heavy pot and an equal amount of water added. This is brought to a boil. The pan is removed from the fire, stirred, and cold water (one quart to four quarts of the hot liquid) added. The cold water precipitates foreign matter and the clean fat floats. The pan is set aside in a cold place, and when the fat becomes firm, it is removed for soap making.

To make soap, a large enamel or iron pot, wider at the top than at the bottom, is necessary. (Lye eats into aluminum, and if the container is narrow at the top, the boiling fat will explode.) A wooden paddle is also needed to stir the lye-and-fat mixture. I remember one year when a dog chewed Mrs. Mahoney's soap stick. We all thought he was rabid as we hung over the fence watching him heave foam.

For a small batch of laundry soap, pour one can of lye into two-and-a-half pints of cold water. Stir until it is dissolved and cool until it is 80° or 85° F.

Melt six pounds of clean soap-making fat until clear and cool it gradually until it has the consistency of egg whites. Stir once in a while during the cooling to prevent fat crystals from forming.

Pour the lye solution slowly into the thickening fat, stirring continuously. The stirring must be smooth, gentle and even, as harsh whipping will cause the fat to separate. As the lye and fat marry, the liquid will become slushy.

After about fifteen or twenty minutes, the sluggish, honey-like soap is poured into a flat wooden box which has been soaked in water and lined with a damp cotton cloth. The wooden box is placed in a protecting box and covered with a cardboard and blanket. This retains the heat and helps to prevent the soap and lye from separating. The soap should not be moved for twenty-four hours.

Soap may be removed from the wooden mold the following day by lifting the ends of the overhanging cotton cloth; then cut into bars with a wire or a stout cord. A knife is not recommended. I once cut soap with the big knife, then cut bread without washing the knife—very bad!

Soap should be aged at room temperature for two weeks but should not be allowed to freeze.

For a stronger soap use six pounds of clean fat, one can of lye, a solution of one-and-a-half tablespoons of borax and two tablespoons of sugar dissolved in a half-cup of warm water, one-half cup of ammonia and two-and-a-half pints of cold water. The fat is melted. When cooled, the lye, dissolved in two-and-a-half pints of cold water (cooled to 80° or 85° F.) is slowly stirred into it. The dissolved borax-sugar solution is gently added, and last, the ammonia is slowly stirred into the mixture. When it reaches the consistency of cold honey, the soap is poured into the mold, cooled, cut and cured.

Floating soap may be made after it reaches the cold-honey stage by folding air into the soap as beaten egg whites are folded into a cake.

Perfumed soap may be made by adding four teaspoons of sassafras extract, or two teaspoons of lavender, or one teaspoon of either citronella, lemon, cloves, almond or rose-geranium extract to the six pounds of fat.

To make soap powder, the bars must be dried (this happens automatically if you store the bars unwrapped) and then grated. A vegetable shredder will make soap flakes from regular moist soap bars.

The real happiness of butchering lies in the making of specialty meats: frankfurters, summer sausage, bologna, Vienna, Westphalian, liver and blood sausage: endless combinations and flavorful results.

A disenchanted German stranded in Anchorage, Alaska, made the finest variety of headcheese, pudding, scrapple and wild sausage that I have ever eaten. When complimented, he used to murmur wryly that he was an "offal artist."

Hund Baur butchered two or three 250-pound porkers every November. Each pig, he said, would dress out to 195 pounds of meat, of which twenty pounds was lean trimmings or "offal."

To make headcheese, or souse, Mr. Baur simmered the pork trimmings (the cleaned, fatless, bony parts of the head containing meat, the hocks, neck and other scraps) until the meat became extremely tender and fell from the bones. He strained out the bones and meat and set the large pan of "solids" aside. The liquid in which they had been boiled was skimmed of any fat, measured and returned to the kettle to boil down by one-half. For every quart of the original liquid (the unreduced liquid in which the pork head and trimmings had been boiled), he added one teaspoon of salt, one-eighth teaspoon of pepper, one chopped onion, one peppercorn, one-half of a crumbled red pepper, one-half bay leaf, one-half blade of mace. The spices were boiled with the liquid, then strained out and the liquid allowed to cool.

While the spice liquid was boiling down, he removed meat from the bones and cut the larger pieces of meat into one-inch squares.

The meat was put into a pan, and for every quart of pork scraps, three-fourths of a cup of vinegar was added. This was brought to a boil, then turned into a mold. Mr. Baur used large enamel cake pans. (My grandmother used crockery headcheese molds.) The hot vinegar-meat was laid level full in each pan and the reduced, spiced liquid was poured over. Then each container was shaken, and as much more liquid as it would hold was added.

Mr. Baur covered and refrigerated his headcheese, then sliced it for sandwich meat. It was jelly clear except for the meat bits and it was beautifully delicate to taste.

My grandmother covered her headcheese with a thin layer of melted lard to seal it. When she wanted some, she scraped the lard away. Headcheese or any uncured variety meat should be kept well covered and refrigerated.

Part of the pork-trimmings meat and the unreduced liquid was made into scrapple by Mr. Bauer. About a quart of the bone-free, finely chopped meat was poured into three cups of the original unreduced, unspiced liquid. Two teaspoons of salt, one-quarter teaspoon of pepper and one teaspoon of ground sage were stirred into the soupy meat mixture and the pan was put over the heat. When the liquid boiled, about one cup of cornmeal was slowly sprinkled over the top and stirred in. As the mixture thickened, it had to be stirred constantly. The fire was lowered and the mushy, plopping scrapple was stirred and cooked for about twenty minutes, then poured into greased loaf pans and quickly cooled.

Scrapple, doused with flour and fried until brown in butter, makes an excellent breakfast when served with toast and boiled apples.

Mr. Baur sometimes made cooked liver sausage, pickled hock loaf, as well as dried and smoked sausages.

My husband and I have tried our hands at home-curing meats and making sausages. Our endeavors were simple, and every piece did not turn out to be top-notch, but we rationalized that total perfection must be boring. Variety is the spice of life, or is it love that spices? In any event, we have had some spicy times and have cured some excellent meats during freeze-up in November.

XII

Days of Rest

DECEMBER-JANUARY

Cutting for grafts under Capricorn. Pruning in Aquarius. Wrap meat to hold. Inventory the cellar: roots, canned, dried and preserved foods checked. Decant and mark wine, blend wines. Catalogs and new garden plans. We are ready for another year. Tomorrow will be February, tomorrow is the beginning.

TIME OF DRUMS, feasts, *wiwik* (games)—time of visiting: the races native to America decreed midwinter as a time of rest.

Cultures close to the land have traditionally provided for a period of relaxation after the harvest and before planting begins again. Although I love a summer vacation, I am all for winter rest, too. My grandfather always said that winter was the only time a man could loaf with an easy conscience.

December and January are considered the coldest months, but in a sense they may also be the warmest. The holy days bring cheer; long, mellow evenings with family or friends bring comfortable pleasures.

Along with baking cookies, wrapping packages and catching the mailman, there are still a few chores to tend during the winter break.

Garden chores are at a minimum. If the strawberries and other perennials have not already been covered with straw, this should be done to protect them.

Grafting fruit trees and vines, moon-sign followers say, should be done during fruitful signs of the moon.

Cut your grafts from good bearing stock while trees and vines are dormant, December to March. Keep the graft branches in a cool, somewhat moist, dark place. Graft onto host plants just before the sap starts to flow.

Moon-sign followers advise grafting while the moon is passing through the fruitful, watery signs of Cancer, Scorpio, Pisces, or the earthy, productive sign of Capricorn, or when specific days are ruled by those signs. They advise that grafting be done while the moon is from new to full (first and second quarters). Do not graft on Sunday, because that day is ruled by the sun and considered dry and barren.

The zodiac period of Capricorn (December 22 to January 20) is said to hold earthy, moist, productive and feminine tendencies. Aquarius (January 20 to February 19) is said to contain airy, dry, barren and masculine characteristics. Accordingly, grafts should be cut under the sign of Capricorn and held to be grafted under Pisces, or on an individual day ruled by Cancer or Scorpio at a time before the sap begins to start upward.

Radical pruning of grapes, moon-sign farmers state, is often done during Capricorn's rule when the moon is in the second quarter. Pruning under the sign of the goat influences new grape vines to reach upward toward the knees, and if they are pruned on the swelling moon, grapes will grow round and juicy.

Pruning fruit trees, however, is said to be most satisfactory when done under a hostile sign such as Aquarius. An orchard man I know prunes the last two weeks of January, and his trees look as if he had given the whole field a crew-cut. Top-pruning trees under a sign hostile to vegetation encourages trees to spread horizontally and grow low to the ground, he said.

The farmer emphasized, however, that if a hostile day sign (daily moon's place) coincides with a zodiac period of dry, barren masculine and fiery characteristics, the result will be extremely rough on growing things. Such a double negative, he said, is only good for killing noxious growths, grubbing and trimming to destroy.

Astrologers state that pruning of fruit trees is best done under the barren sign of Aquarius, on days that are not doubly hostile to vegetation, but when the moon is in the last quarter.

Apples, pears and root crops should be checked regularly under the moist sign of Capricorn, my grandfather said, because they deteriorate rapidly at that time. If they show signs of breakdown, they should be eaten or canned.

Hanging pork and sausage should be watched carefully for

signs of deterioration under Capricorn, but if possible should be held until Aquarius for wrapping. Aquarius' dry characteristics will hold meat, my grandfather believed.

Pork which has been put down in salt-sugar cure and hung to dry should be wrapped when thoroughly dry to protect it against rancidness and insects.

My grandfather wrapped his cured and dried meat in parchment paper and sacked it in clean muslin. He then wrapped each ham in brown paper and hung the pork in a dry, cool, airy, dark area of the cellar. Sometimes he rubbed the hams which were to be kept over the summer with corn syrup and black and red pepper before wrapping, and he painted the outside of the wrapping paper with lime mixed with dry glue and water. This chalky coating discouraged insects and spoilage, he said. He always hung the meat by an outside string that did not touch the meat. A newer method of wrapping meat is to cover each piece with cheesecloth or unbleached muslin, then tie the meat tightly in brown paper and put the pieces into grocery bags.

Every month or so, home-cured pork should be checked for skippers, mites and beetles. Insects may be controlled by trimming the affected meat and rewrapping. The storage area should be scrubbed with hot, soapy water and kept free from flies and ants, which carry mites.

Because they are more apt to crack and become rancid, bacon and shoulders should be eaten first.

Beef does not keep as well as pork, so beef put down in dry cure or pickle should be used before the hams. Corned beef may be held in its own pickle or refrigerated after it is cured.

Dried or smoked fish should be eaten before March because they tend to become rancid toward spring. Moon-sign followers say that the watery sign of Pisces beckons fish; they "throw their cure" and try to return to the sea.

December and January are the months to inventory canned vegetables and to note the less popular items. Lining up the canned foods tells me those which should be "pushed" for the table. During the canning season I usually shove jars any place they will fit; often it is after Christmas before I organize the cellar.

During midwinter I also check jams and jellies for variety and to see if they are weeping. "A little mold won't hurt jelly," my grandmother used to say, but I try to reparaffin jars that show moisture.

Potatoes and other root crops should be checked and picked over for softness. Onions, if you have any, should be used up; they do not keep well as spring approaches.

Herbs and teas, as well as dried foods, may profit from a ten-minute hitch in a low oven to discourage mildew.

After the first of the year, pumpkins and squash must be watched carefully because as the days lengthen, they are likely to show signs of rot.

If you have kraut or pickles in crocks, add saline solution if they are losing too much juice.

December and January mark the ripening of many wines. Although most wines mature and become fuller with age, wine six or seven months old is not too young to nip. I decant wine before the holidays so that the wine will clear before it is to be drunk.

Homemade wines usually contain a degree of sediment. Even after settling in the crock, and careful pouring into storage containers, and decanting into small bottles in December, solids remain at the bottom. My grandmother poured the last glassful of the decanted wine into a cruet for cooking and repeatedly emphasized that wine must be handled carefully and not shaken.

To hold bouquet and flavor, I reseal all rebottled wine. I have also learned that decanted wine should be labeled. I remember bringing a bottle of topaz daisy to a bridal reception—a toast to the bride. Happiness and love, symbol of the daisy. The wine turned out to be yellow dandelion and tasted exactly like dandelion greens. I worried about that marriage;

some gardeners consider the dandelion a floral delinquent.

December decanting tells you what you've got and how much. My husband likes to reconnoiter in the cellar; it stimulates his security senses, he says.

Blending wine calls for courage and creativity. Some cock-eyed and superior surprises result.

The steps are simple: 1. Decant. 2. Sniff and sip. 3. Breathe deeply, eyes closed, and think. 4. Categorize (dry, sweet, acid, *ugh*). 5. Ask yourself, What does this wine tell me? 6. Objectively question its faults (a second sip and sniff may be needed). 7. How can it be improved? A drop of color, a little more head? 8. Does it grab you?

One of my neighbors rates her wines from Unsatisfactory to Outstanding, with the adjectives Poor, Satisfactory, Good, Very Good and Excellent in between. She also rates acidity, aftertaste, aroma, balance, body, bouquet, clarity, color, smoothness, and taste on a scale of I, II, III, IV. She says this evaluation gives her an accurate picture of which wines to blend. My blending is spontaneous, hers is scientific.

Although commercial wine blending is a highly regarded skill, blending homemade wine is a personal pursuit. A purist would shudder at blending daisy with roots, or honeysuckle with crab apple, but my husband and I enjoy a trip to the basement to blend. Sometimes we create a terrific combination and other times the sink backs up when we pour it out. Even the plumbing refuses to drink our concoction.

Cork inspection is a chore for December–January. On the whole, corks are untrustworthy. They shrink, weep, leak, and some, I believe, drink wine. Humidity and cork shrinkage are related. If the humidity of the wine-storage area is not high enough, corks will dry out and shrink. Even those coated with paraffin sometimes need replacing.

Some wine makers keep a diary of wines on hand. They then choose the precise beverage they desire. That sounds like a good idea, but my approach is more casual. Light, dark, sweet, dry; each has its own corner. I close my eyes and reach for the corner I want. Of course, sometimes we have peach with chicken when elder blow would have been better, but more often it's like getting a baby. You are all set for one with inside plumbing, the other kind arrives, and you love it.

My grandfather brought up from the cellar the wine he "felt like." If he felt like elderberry, that was the one we drank. If he felt like cherry or calf-feed (made from corn, wheat, rye, and raisins), no one complained; oddball wine eliminates menu monotony.

After the holidays, when thank-you notes and goodies are gone, it is refreshing to sit and browse through seed catalogs. It is a time to dream of garden happinesses and to hope. I can become so enthusiastic amid my catalogs on a snowy day that I hear doves and jays, smell the earth, and yearn to feel the soil. New varieties of seed must be studied and compared with old standby seeds. Different kinds of plantings must be considered. I make up a garden plan on paper; then we all get into the act.

Martin chooses the tomatoes, Penny is our bean girl and Lewis picks the corn. Every year we hold a pow-wow and each speaks up for his chosen planting location and seed; each argues with vigor. Then I redo the garden plan, Marie makes out the order, and Lewis writes a check. We are ready for another year.

Tomorrow will be February, I remind myself as I race for the mailman. "Seeds Swell," "First Things Are Born," "River Mothers Grow Big." . . . Tomorrow is the beginning.

XIII

Rules of the Game
General Information

Season for all things. Save. Poisonous wild plants listed. Rules of wine making. Rules of the garden game. Garden-planting chart. Zodiac signs and their periods. Canning rules. Storage rules. Rules of the meat-curing game. The cardinal rule is to live in harmony throughout the natural year.

THE BEAUTY of all nature lies in its versatile rhythm.

There is a time for all things.
—Shakespeare,
Comedy of Errors, Act II, Scene 2

*. . . there is a season, and a time to every purpose under
the heaven.*
—Ecclesiastes III

But absolutes in nature are rare. Some years you get beans;
other seasons, frogs' legs grow meaty. There is no guarantee
that poke will be ready to cut in May or that it will be cold
enough to butcher in November.

During a natural year, the first rule of your personal game
is to stay loose. Forage wild foods, put down a little wine,
scratch the soil, keep an eye on the moon and tides, hunt, fish,
preserve, enjoy the life and save.

The cardinal rule of all natural years is *Save.* Save the
earth's life and beauties; save its goodnesses; respect all of
God's creations; save love for fellow man.

Scientific truths and absolutes are fine; folklore and fancies
are fun. During a natural year science and lore are not mutu-
ally exclusive. Legends and fancies reign in some areas, science is supreme in others.

The area in which science reigns absolute, however, is in
the realm of poisonous plants.

Wild plants, unless positively identified as edible, should
never be eaten.

Wild plants should be eaten only as directed. Some plants
are poisonous when eaten raw but wholesome when cooked;
some bear edible fruit but the roots and leaves are poisonous;
some plants may be eaten only in the young sprouting stage,

others are edible only when dried. A forager need not be a botanist, but explicit care should be taken to identify edible species of plants and to gather them at the proper stage.

Several hundred plants found throughout the United States and Canada are known to have caused illness or death among those who ate them. Poisonous plants likely to be mistaken for edible ones should be studied and identified in their natural habitat.

A good handbook on edible wild plants and association with people who regularly eat wild foods are both essential for successful and pleasurable foraging. Write to your state wildlife commission for a pamphlet on edible and poisonous plants of your state.

Here is a list of plants sufficiently poisonous in whole or in part as to be named "dangerous."

DANGEROUS

Poisonous Rootstocks or Bulbs

Atamasco lily (*Zephyranthes atamasco*)
Bloodroot (*Sanguinaria canadensis*)
Blue Flag (*Iris versicolor*)
Butterfly-weed (*Asclepias tuberosa*)
Cowbane (*Oxypolis rigidior*)
Death-camass (*Zigadenus anticlea*)
Fly-poison (*Anianthium muscaetoxicum*)
Mayapple (*Podophyllum peltatum*)
Pokeweed (*Phytolacca americana*)
Red-root (*Lachnanthes tinctoria*)
Star-of-Bethlehem (*Ornithogalum umbellatum*)
Water-hemlock, and bulb-bearing water-hemlock (*Cicuta maculata* and *Cicuta bulbifera*)
White Snakeroot (*Eupatorium urticaefolium, Eupatorium rugosum*)

Poisonous Plant Sprouts, New Shoots, Spikes or Young Leaves

Boxwood (*Buxus sempervirens*)
Buttercup (*Ranunculus acris*)

Castor-bean (*Ricinus communis*)
Cherry, Peach and Plum (*Prunus*)
Devil's-bit (*Chamaelirium luteum*)
Dogbane (*Apocynum*)
Fool's-parsley (*Aethusa cynapium*)
Hemp (*Cannabis sativa*)
Horse-tail (*Equisetum*)
Indian poke, or white hellebore (*Veratrum viride*)
Jewel-weed (*Impatiens*)
Jimson-weed (*Datura stramonium*)
Marsh marigold (*Caltha palustris*)
Mexican tea (*Chenopodium ambrosioides*)
Milkweed (*Asclepias*)
Nightshade (*Solanum dulcamara*)
Pimpernel (*Anagallis arvensis*)
Poison hemlock (*Conium maculatum*)
Velvet grass (*Holcus lanatus*)
Wild indigo (*Baptisia*)
Yellow Jessamine (*Gelsemium sempervirens*)
Yew (*Taxus canadensis*)

Poisonous Fruits and Seeds

Arrow-grass (*Triglochin*)
Buckeye or Horse-chestnut (*Aesculus*)
Burning-bush (*Euonymus atropurpureus*)
Castor-bean (*Ricinus communis*)
Corn-cockle (*Argrostemma githago*)
Henbane (*Hyoscyamus niger*)
Hoary-pea (*Tephrosia*)
Jimson-weed (*Datura stramonium*)
Kentucky coffee-tree (*Gymnocladus dioicus*)
Locust (*Robinia*)
Lupines (*Lupinus perennis*)
Rattle-box (*Crotalaria*)
Spurges (*Euphorbia*)
Vetches (*Vicia*)

Poisonous Berries

Baneberry, red or white (*Actaea rubra* or *alba*)
Beautyberry (*Callicarpa*)
Bittersweet (*Solanum dulcamara*)
Black-berried nightshade (*Solanum nigrum*)
Buckthorn (*Rhamnus*)
English Ivy (*Hedera helix*)

Poisonous Berries (Cont.)
>   Ground-hemlock (*Taxus canadensis*)
>   Melonette (*Melothria pendula*)
>   Mistletoe (*Phoradendron flavescens*)
>   Moonseed (*Menispermum candense*)
>   Pride-of-Indian tree (*Melia azedarach*)
>   Privet (*Ligustrum vulgare*)

Wild mushrooms should not be eaten unless the forager is absolutely certain of their identity.

The first rule of home wine making in the United States is to secure a permit. Each fiscal year (July 1–June 30) you must write to the Treasury Department for an Internal Revenue form number 1541 entitled "Registration for Production of Wine for Family Use." The IRS permits a household head to make two hundred gallons of wine each year after the duplicate of Form 1541 has been filled out and returned. A home wine maker must promise not to sell wine or make wine in partnership.

A second rule of wine making is cleanliness. Fruits, blossoms and commercial yeasts cause fermentation, but in order to restrict the growth of yeasts that secrete sour enzymes, sterile procedures should be followed or potassium metabisulphate should be added.

Wine goes through several fermentation periods: with the fruit, after the fruit has been strained from the juice, and in containers with airlocks or bottles lightly corked.

Rule of thumb for the use of sugar in winemaking is to use two-and-a-half pounds of sugar per gallon of liquid. Tart fruits may utilize more sugar, pallid petals require a minimum of sugar. Sugar partially determines the alcoholic content of wine. (Two-and-a-half pounds of sugar per gallon will usually produce 14 percent of alcohol by volume.) But alcohol destroys yeasts and stops fermentation after 16 or 18 percent alcohol by volume has been achieved. Too much sugar will turn into too-sweet wine.

A hydrometer is a useful tool in the second fermentation

step of wine making because, simply stated, it measures how much sugar a liquid contains and how much has been used up. The more sugar a liquid contains, the higher a hydrometer will float. As yeasts use up sugars the hydrometer sinks; thus, as hydrometer readings become lower, fermentation slows and wine should be watched for the action to stop and the bottling time to begin.

A thermometer is another important tool in wine making. Fermenting temperatures should be kept in the 60°–80° F. range. Wine should be stored at 50° F.

Earthenware, glass, stone, enamel, plastic or wooden vessels are used in wine making because some metal containers react to the acid in wines.

"Bite" is achieved through ginger root, peppercorns or cassia buds.

Wines may be cleared by settling and siphoning off the top wine; one eggshell may be crumbled into the liquid; or one ounce of glycerine may be added per gallon of wine before the final bottling.

Fill and seal containers used in wine storage because air spoils most wines and corks shrink.

Wine may be made from most edible fruits. Do not use unknown fruits or flower petals. Some fruits, such as buckthorn, and some flowers, such as buttercups, foxglove and lilac, can produce violently poisonous potions.

Pick fruits and flowers from plants that have not been sprayed with insecticides.

Use only positively identified and known substances in winemaking.

The first rule of the garden game is to keep telling yourself that gardening is fun.

Most vegetables respond best to sunshine and well-drained humus-type soil. Avoid shade. Run rows north and south, if practical.

Proper soil preparation cuts down on summer cultivating chores. Garden soil should be moist at planting time to germinate most seeds.

Use certified seed. Be generous with favorite vegetables.

Vegetables are heavy feeders. Fertilize properly for success with them.

Hoe or scrape to destroy weeds as soon as they appear because they sap nutrients and moisture from the garden.

Mulch two inches deep, or use black polyethylene film with slits for moisture seepage, wherever practical.

Bugs and fungus diseases destroy vegetables; control them early—by nonpoisonous methods, if possible.

Grow an oddball plant or two for fun.

Add interest with herbs.

Perennial vegetables such as asparagus and rhubarb can be a special pleasure in a home vegetable garden.

For those people who garden by the moon, it is believed that each constellation has wet or dry tendencies and barren or productive characteristics. When the moon is in the barren signs of Gemini, Leo or Virgo, moon-sign followers destroy noxious growth, deaden trees, pull weeds and turn sod, especially if the moon is in the last quarter.

Planting is said to be best done in the fruitful or productive signs of Scorpio, Pisces, Taurus or Cancer. In addition, astrologers say that it is best to plant all things that yield above ground in the increase of the moon, and all things that yield below ground when the moon is decreasing.

Planting or grafting done on Sunday, moon-sign believers say, will probably not succeed, as this day is ruled by the sun and therefore considered to be a dry and barren day.

As the zodiacal sign Libra represents beauty in form and color, it is considered the best for flowers. The seeds should be planted in the first quarter of the moon unless seeds from the plant are desired, in which case use the period between the second quarter and the full moon.

Harvest all crops when the moon is growing old, astrologers

Garden Planting Chart
Mid-Atlantic States

Vegetable	Seed or Plants for 100 Feet of Row	Time of Seeding or Transplanting	Days Ready After Seeding or Transplanting
Beet	1 oz.	March to Aug. 15	45–62
Broccoli	50–60 plants	March to July	75–100
Brussels sprouts	66 plants	March to July	90–100
Cabbage	75 plants	March to July	65–120
Carrot	½ oz.	March to July 15	55–80
Chard, Swiss	1 oz.	March to Aug.	40–60
Corn, sweet	4 oz.	April to July 15	60–95
Cucumber	½ oz.	May and Aug.	50–75
Eggplant	50 plants	May	80–100
Endive	1 oz.	March and July	80–90
Green pea	1 lb.	Feb. to Mar.	50–75
Kale	½ oz.	March and Aug.	55–70
Lettuce	¼ oz.	March and July	43–85
Lima bean	8–12 oz.	May and June	65–75
Muskmelon	½ oz.	May	80–100
Okra	1½ oz.	May to Aug.	55–65
Onion sets	2 lb.	March and April	40–100
Parsley	½ oz.	March and April	60–90
Parsnip	½ oz.	March and April	100–130
Pepper	66 plants	May	60–95
Potato	6 lb.	March	100–120
Pumpkin	½ oz.	May	90–120
Radish	1 oz.	March to Oct.	20–75
Salsify	1 oz.	April to May	130–150
Snap bean	12–16 oz.	April to Aug.	42–60
Snap bean, pole	10 oz.	April to May	60–80
Spinach	1½ oz.	March and April	40–50
Squash, summer	½ oz.	May and July	45–70
Squash, winter	½ oz.	May and June	82–110
Sweet potato	100 plants	May and June	110–135
Tomato	50 plants	May and June	62–95
Turnip	½ oz.	March and Aug.	45–90
Upland cress	½ oz.	August	55
Watermelon	1 oz.	May	72–120

advise, except grains intended for future seed. These should be harvested at the increase of the moon.

ZODIAC SIGNS AND THEIR PERIODS

AQUARIUS—January 20 to February 19. Airy, dry and barren.

PISCES—February 19 to March 21. Watery and fruitful.

ARIES—March 21 to April 20. Fiery, dry and barren.

TAURUS—April 20 to May 21. Earthy, moist and productive.

GEMINI—May 21 to June 21. Airy, dry and barren.

CANCER—June 21 to July 22. Watery and very fruitful.

LEO—July 22 to August 23. Fiery, barren and dry.

VIRGO—August 23 to September 23. Earthy, dry and barren.

LIBRA—September 23 to October 23. Airy, moist and semi-fruitful.

SCORPIO—October 23 to November 22. Watery and fruitful.

SAGITTARIUS—November 22 to December 22. Fiery, dry and barren.

CAPRICORN—December 22 to January 20. Earthy, moist, productive.

The rules of the game in canning fruits and vegetables in a boiling-water bath apply to both hot and cold pack. First, plan to donate a whole day to canning. Half of the work in canning is rounding up the utensils, and once into production it is best to can all produce that is ready. Jelly making may be done in dibs and dabs, but canning is an all-day operation.

Inspect jars and caps for perfect sealing edges. They must be clean, sterilized and kept in hot water until ready for use.

The actual number of jars needed depends upon the produce, preparation and manner of packing. As a rule of thumb:

BEETS   1 bu. (50 lb.)—17 to 20 quart jars needed.
CORN   1 bu. (35 lb.)—8 to 9 quart jars needed.
PEAS   1 bu. (30 lb.)—6 to 7 quart jars needed.
SNAP BEANS   1 bu. (30 lb.)—15 to 20 quart jars needed.
SPINACH   1 bu. (18 lb.)—6 to 9 quart jars needed.
SQUASH, SUMMER   1 bu (40 lbs.)—16 to 20 quart jars needed.

Tomatoes 1 bu. (50 lb.)—18 to 22 quart jars needed.
Apples 1 bu. (50 lb.)—15 to 20 quart jars needed.
Applesauce 1 bu. (50 lb.)—15 to 18 quart jars needed.
Berries (can into about one-half of raw measure) 12 quarts—6 to 7 quart jars needed.
Peaches 1 bu. (50 lb.)—18 to 24 quart jars needed.
Pears 1 bu. (50 lb.)—20 to 24 quart jars needed.
Plums 1 bu. (55 lb.)—25 to 30 quart jars needed.

Select firm, sound fruits and vegetables and wash thoroughly before canning. Whole fruit that has not been peeled must be punctured with a needle to prevent the skin from bursting. Blanching is a quick way to remove skins from tomatoes, peaches and other fruits. Immerse fruit in boiling water for one or two minutes, drain and cover with cold water to permit handling, then peel. Process immediately.

Pack food solidly into containers. Cover solid food with boiling water, syrup or liquid from precooking, and work out the air bubbles with a knife blade.

Allow one inch of head space for starchy foods and one-half inch of head space for acid vegetables and fruits.

Add one teaspoonful of salt for each quart after packing vegetables into the jars.

Clean lips of jars and, if self-sealing lids are used, screw caps tight before putting the jars into the boiling-water bath.

Keep the water boiling in the canner during processing.

Remove the jars from the canner as soon as the time is up. Do not touch lids on self-sealing-type caps.

Before storing, keep samples at room temperature for two days to check seal and condition of the fruit.

Inspect canned food before eating. Discard any fruit that is discolored or has an unnatural odor. Do not taste food to determine spoilage.

Store canned goods in a cool, darkened area that is convenient for daily use.

Storage facilities for fresh fruits and vegetables should be clean, darkened if possible, somewhat moist, and cool.

Dry beans and peas, corn and hominy may be kept in any

cool, dry place after they have been heated in a low oven (180° to 200° F.) for thirty minutes.

Late cabbage, onions, apples and pears may be kept separately through early winter at temperatures close to 32° F.

Potatoes may be kept until spring in a darkened storage area at temperature of 35° F.

Pumpkins, squash and sweet potatoes may be kept through early winter in a dry, dark place with temperature near 55° F.

Tomatoes like the warm life and, if wrapped, may be kept six to eight weeks with temperatures in the sixties.

The rules of the game for keeping cured meats are simple. Keep the meat dry, cool, well ventilated, away from direct light, pieces separated from each other, and in a screened storage area.

Bacon is usually best shortly after it comes from the cure, and most people prefer to use up the bacon during the spring and early summer. Fat meat gets rancid quicker than lean meat.

Shoulders should be used up before the hams, because hams usually improve with age.

Cured beef and mutton do not keep as well as cured pork, and therefore should be used sooner.

Regardless of the kind of meat or the way it was cured, proper storage is necessary if the meat is to be kept in good condition for any length of time.

Dried, smoked, salted or pickled fish should be stored in a dry, cool, well-aired place, preferably not in direct light, and, depending on the strength of cure, they should be used before early winter.

Fishing laws, tide tables and charts should be studied prior to a trip to the shore.

Local regulations regarding game should be checked before planning a hunt. Rules for care of firearms should be observed. Game should be properly bled and dressed.

The rules of the game are infinite.

But the primary rules—to live in harmony with God's laws and with one's fellow men; to live in harmony with the earth's plants, its tides, air, matter, and creatures; to live in harmony with all nature—add up to living a natural year.

Bibliography

EDIBLE PLANTS

Beck, Barbara. *The First Book of Weeds*. New York: Franklin Watts, 1963.

Carver, George W. *Nature's Garden for Victory and Peace*, Bulletin No. 43, Tuskegee Institute. Tuskegee, Ala.: Tuskegee Institute Press, 1942.

Fernald, Merrit L., Kinsey, A. C., and Rollins, Reed C. *Edible Wild Plants of Eastern North America*, revised edition. New York: Harper and Row, 1958.

Gibbons, Euell. *Stalking the Wild Asparagus*. New York: David McKay, 1962.

Grimm, William C. *Recognizing Native Shrubs*. Harrisburg, Pa.: Stackpole Books, 1966.

Hardy, G. A. *Edible Plants of British Columbia*. Bulletin No. 1. Victoria, B.C.: British Columbia Museum, 1942.

Peterson, Roger Tory, and McKenny, Margaret. *A Field Guide to Wildflowers*. Boston: Houghton Mifflin, 1968.

Petrides, G. A. *A Field Guide to Trees and Shrubs*. Boston: Houghton Mifflin, 1958.

Porsild, A. E. "Edible Plants of the Arctic," *Arctic*, Vol. VI (March 1953).

Sharples, Ada. *Alaskan Wildflowers*. 1938.

"Spring Greens," *Successful Farming*. May 1946.

Taylor, Raymond C. *Plants of Colonial Days*. Williamsburg, Va.: Williamsburg Press, 1952.

POISONOUS PLANTS

Massey, A. B. "Poisonous Plants in Virginia," *Virginia Wildlife*. Richmond, Va.: Commission of Game and Inland Fisheries, February 1959.

Kingsbury, John M. *Poisonous Plants of the United States and Canada*. Englewood Cliffs, N.J.: Prentice-Hall, 1964.

HERBS

David, Elizabeth. *Spices, Salt and Aromatics in the English Kitchen*. Harmondsworth, Middlesex: Penguin Books Ltd., 1970.

Doyle, Louise Evans. *Herbs, How to Grow and Use Them*. New York: Sterling Publishers, 1962.
Lust, Benedict. *About Herbs*. London: Thorsons Publishers, Ltd., 1968.
Ranson, Florence. *British Herbs*. Harmondsworth, Middlesex: Penguin Books Ltd., 1954.
Sheldon, Ferne. *Colonial Kitchen Herbs*. High Point, N.C.: Hutcraft, 1970.

MOON LORE

Farmers' Almanac. Lewiston, Maine: Almanac Publishing Co., 1968.
Gibson, Walter B. and Litzka R. *The Complete Illustrated Book of the Psychic Sciences*. Garden City, N.Y.: Doubleday & Co., 1966.
Grier's Almanac. Atlanta, Georgia: Grier's Almanac Publishing Co., 1969–71.
Hagerstown Town and Country Almanack. Nos. CXXI–CLXXIV. Hagerstown, Md.: The Gruber Almanack Co., 1918–1971.
Old Farmers' Almanac. Dublin, N.H.: Yankee Inc., 1970.
Warrock-Richardson Almanack. Richmond, Va.: Clyde W. Sanders and Sons, Inc., 1941.
Weschcke, Carl. *Moon Sign Book*. St. Paul, Minnesota: Llewellyn Publishers, 1970.
Wright, Hamilton and Helen, and Rapport, Samuel (eds.). *To the Moon*. New York: Meredith Press, 1968.

BREAD, YEAST AND WINE

Bravery, H. E. *Home Brewing*. New York: Gramercy Publishers, 1965.
Herter, George Leonard. *Finest Wines*. Waseca, Minn.: Herter Publications, 1969.
Homemade Bread. Bulletin 1775. Washington: U.S. Dept. of Agriculture, 1942.
Kavaler, Lucy. *Mushrooms, Molds and Miracles*. New York: John Day, 1965.
Sichel, Allan. *Wines*. Harmondsworth, Middlesex: Penguin Books Ltd., 1965.

VEGETABLE GARDENING

Bissell, T. L. and Ditman, L. P. *Insect Control on Vegetable Crops*. Extension Bulletin 199. College Park, Md.: U.S. Dept. of Agriculture, 1966.
Carleton, R. Milton, *Vegetables for Today's Gardens*. New York: Van Nostrand Reinhold Company, 1967.

Bibliography

Everett, Thomas H. (ed.) *Complete Book of the Garden*. Pleasantville, N.Y.: The Reader's Digest Association, Inc., 1966.

Handbook of Agronomy, Bulletin 97. Blacksburg, Va.: Virginia Polytechnic Institute, 1956.

Hunter, Beatrice T. *Gardening Without Poisons*. Boston: Houghton Mifflin, 1964.

Hunter, Herman A. and Charles W. Reynolds. *Vegetable Gardening*. Extension Bulletin 220. College Park, Md.: U.S. Dept. of Agriculture, 1967.

"New Dope for Old Bugs," *The Farm Journal*, Philadelphia. August 1933.

Rodale, J. I. (ed.) *The Encyclopedia of Organic Gardening*. Emmaus, Pa.: Rodale Books Inc., 1965.

"Ten Little Insects," *Successful Farming*, Des Moines, Iowa. July 1946.

Thomas, F. L. "Non-Poisonous Insecticides for Use on Vegetable Crops," *Market Growers Journal*, Louisville, Ky. January 15, 1936.

COOKING

Harland, Marion. *Marion Harland's Complete Cookbook*. Indianapolis: Bobbs-Merrill Co., 1903.

Montagne, Prosper. *Larousse Gastronomique*. New York: Crown Publishers, Inc., 1965.

Tyree, Marion Cabell (ed.) *Housekeeping in Old Virginia*. Louisville, Ky.: John P. Morgan and Co., 1879.

CANNING AND PRESERVING

Apple Cider. U.S. Dept. of Agriculture, Farmers' Bulletin 2125. Washington: Government Printing Office, 1967.

Ball Blue Book, Home Canning. Muncie, Indiana: Ball Brothers Inc., 1956.

Home Canning. U.S. Dept. of Agriculture, Home and Garden Bulletin 8. Washington: Government Printing Office, 1965.

How to Make Jellies, Jams and Preserves at Home. U.S. Dept. of Agriculture, Home and Garden Bulletin 56. Washington: Government Printing Office, 1967.

Making Pickles and Relishes at Home. U.S. Dept. of Agriculture, Home and Garden Bulletin 92. Washington: Government Printing Office, 1967.

Storing Vegetables and Fruits. U.S. Dept. of Agriculture, Home and Garden Bulletin 119. Washington: Government Printing Office, 1970.

MEATS AND FISH

Gibbon, Euell. *Stalking the Blue-Eyed Scallop.* New York: David Mc-Kay, 1964.

Home Meat Curing. Chicago (110 N. Wacker Drive): Morton Salt Company, 1969.

"How to Make Soap at Home." *Successful Farming*, Des Moines, Iowa. February 1947.

"Making Sausage." *Successful Farming*, Des Moines, Iowa. November 1942.

Pheil, Judith A. *Maryland Seafood.* College Park, Md.: University of Maryland Extension Service, 1962.

Processing Beef on the Farm. U.S. Dept. of Agriculture, Farmers' Bulletin 2209. Washington: Government Printing Office, 1965.

Processing Pork on the Farm. U.S. Dept. of Agriculture, Farmers' Bulletin 2138. Washington: Government Printing Office, 1967.

Tide Tables. U.S. Dept. of Commerce, Coast and Geodetic Survey. Rockville, Md.: Coast and Geodetic Environmental Service, 1971.

Index

Acorn bread, 31
Acorn coffee, 169
Acorus calamus, 47
Allium family, 51
Amaranth, 50, 60
Amelanchier, 105
Apios americana, 145
Apocynum androsaemifolium, 81
Apple(s), 139-140, 179-184, 224
   butter, 182
   fried, 140
   peeling wine, 139
   sauce, 139
Aquarius, 21-22, 224-225, 238
Aralia nudicaulis, 153
Arenaria peploides, 53
Aries, 41-42, 57, 238
Armoracia lapathifolia, 59
Asarum canadensis, 194
Asclepias syriaca, 81, 149
Asimina triloba, 147
Asparagus, 43, 82-83

Baked-appleberry, 122
Barbarea vulgaris, 171
Basil, 43, 166
Bayberry, 190
Betula lenta, 128, 151
Blackberry-dewberry, 122-126
   canned, 126
   cordial, 124
   dried, 125-126
   jam, 124-125
   pie, 125
Blueberry, 126
Borage, 166
Bracken, 83
Brassica, 59

Bread
   acorn, 31
   brown, 30
   lima bean, 30
   sponge method of making, 28-29
   straight dough method, 28
   white, 28-29
Burnet, 166

Cabbage, 22, 42, 73, 97, 121, 240
   sauerkraut, 136-137
Cakile edentula, 60
Cancer, 44, 93-94, 118, 238
Candy
   ginger root, 194
   horehound, 193
   spearmint, 193
   taffy, 193
   wintergreen, 193
Canning, 122, 238-239
   best moon signs for, 53
   blackberries, 126
   green beans, 121
   mincemeat, 187
   mushrooms, 80
   peas, 102
   sauerkraut, 136-137
   sausage, 214
   tomatoes, 159
   wild greens, 53
Capricorn, 223-225, 238
Capsella bursa-pastoris, 50
Caraway, 43, 167
Cassia occidentalis, 169
Catfish, 46
Cattails, 44-46, 187
Checkerberry, 190

Index

Index

Slippery elm, 26
Smartweed, 190
Smoking (of fish)
  cold-, 67
  Hot-, 68
Smoking chambers, 67
Soap, 216-218
Sorrel, 190
Sourdough starter, 27
Spicebush
  condiment, 190
  tea, 128
Sprouts, wild edible, 80-83
Squash, 58, 75, 119
  summer, 103
  winter, 185, 237
Storage, 239
  apples, 179
  meat, 225
  potatoes, 158, 226
  roots, 185
  sweet potatoes, 158
  tomatoes, 186
  winter squash, 185
Strawberry, 44, 76-79
  ice cream, 78
  muffins, 77-78
  wild, 76
  wine, 79
Sumacade, 151
Sweet birch
  cooler, 151
  herb, 190
  tea, 128
Sweet cicely, 191
Sweet coltsfoot, 53
Sweet-flag, 47
Sweetgale, 191
Symplocarpus foetidus, 52

Tansy, 191
Tarragon, 167
Taurus, 58, 73, 238
Tea, 127-129
  elder, 110, 129
  medicinal, 87

rose petal, 85
sassafras, 128
slippery elm, 26
spice bush, 128
sweet birch, 128
yaupon, 129
Thlaspi arvense, 59
Thyme, 144, 168
Tomato(es), 23, 73
  canned, 159
  catsup, 160
  green relish, 160
  storage of, 186
Tragopogon, 52
Turtle, snapping, 95-97
Typha latifolia, 187

Ulmus fulva, 26
Urtica, 152

Vaccinium, 126, 195
Venison, 207-209
Veratrum viride, 52, 232
Vinegar, 37
Virgo, 157, 238
Vitis labrusca, 146
Vitis rotundifolia, 171

Watermelon rind pickles, 161
Weather predictions, 117-118
White hellebore, 52, 232
Wine, 234
  beet, 34
  blackberry, 123
  blending, 227
  carrot, 35
  cranberry, 195
  daisy, 83-84
  honeysuckle, 84
  mulligan, 36
  permit for making, 234
  perry, 206

252